Good Governance Is a Choice

"Practical. Understandable. Doable. The approach in this book on governance is written without jargon and contrived language and concepts."

—*Kathy L. Smith, chair, Fairfax County Public Schools, VA*

"This book is a tremendous resource for us to reference, especially with board and superintendent turnover."

— *Laura Kornasiewicz, Aspen School District board member, CO*

"This work focuses the board and district on authentic results for student achievement and the data necessary for the board to know its standards are being met."

—*Lorri McCune, superintendent of Palm Springs Unified School District, CA*

"This book delineates true governing authority, appropriate delegation to professional staff to actually do their jobs, and rigorous accountability."

—*Bill Van Atta, president of the Racine Unified School District Board of Education, WI and Global Sales and Marketing Process Director, S. C. Johnson & Son, Inc.*

Good Governance Is a Choice

A Way to Re-create Your Board—the *Right* Way

RANDY QUINN AND LINDA J. DAWSON

ROWMAN & LITTLEFIELD EDUCATION
A Division of
ROWMAN & LITTLEFIELD PUBLISHERS, INC.
Lanham • New York • Toronto • Plymouth, UK

Published by Rowman & Littlefield Education
A division of Rowman & Littlefield Publishers, Inc.
A wholly owned subsidiary of The Rowman & Littlefield Publishing Group, Inc.
4501 Forbes Boulevard, Suite 200, Lanham, Maryland 20706
http://www.rowmaneducation.com

Estover Road, Plymouth PL6 7PY, United Kingdom

British Library Cataloguing in Publication Information Available

Library of Congress Cataloging-in-Publication Data
Quinn, Randy.
  Good governance is a choice : a way to re-create your board the right way / Randy Quinn and Linda J. Dawson.
     p. cm.
  ISBN 978-1-61048-312-4 (cloth : alk. paper) — ISBN 978-1-61048-313-1 (pbk. : alk. paper) — ISBN 978-1-61048-314-8 (electronic)
  1. School boards. 2. School board-superintendent relationships. I. Dawson, Linda J., 1952- II. Title.
  LB2831.Q46 2011
  379.1'531—dc22

                                                                    2010051419

∞™ The paper used in this publication meets the minimum requirements of American National Standard for Information Sciences—Permanence of Paper for Printed Library Materials, ANSI/NISO Z39.48-1992.

Printed in the United States of America

Contents

Foreword   vii

Preface   ix

1   Why Don't Boards Perform Better?   1

2   What Does a High-Performing Board Look Like?   9

3   Governing Coherently or Incoherently?   17

4   Constructing the Board's Own Governing Culture   27

5   The Board's Relationship with Its CEO—Part 1   37

6   Controlling Operational Decisions without Helping the
    CEO Manage   41

7   Becoming a Results-Driven Organization   57

8   The Board's Relationship with Its CEO—Part 2   65

9   Monitoring—Everything!   71

10 Systemic Application and Alignment   81

11 Governing Coherently: How Can a Board Transform Itself?   87

Appendix A: Board Self-Assessment   93

Appendix B: Operational Expectations Monitoring Report   95

Appendix C: Results Monitoring Report   113

Appendix D: Summative CEO Evaluation   133

Glossary   139

About the Authors   143

Foreword

This is a book on board governance that I wish I had written. But if I had, it would not have been nearly as good as it is.

Why? The book's authors, Dr. Randy Quinn and Linda J. Dawson, not only are recognized across our nation as some of the most effective board trainers in America, but they also have lifetimes of experiences in the actual governance and executive management of large, complex organizations serving volunteer, elected members of governmental entities in our American democratic culture.

Their viewpoints about how boards should operate are not offered as observers from some distant ivory tower. Their views are absolutely realistic and practical, formulated by two highly intelligent and well-educated people based upon their long working careers dealing with the real-life challenges that boards face.

The authors have dealt firsthand with the whole spectrum of differing personalities who serve on boards of all types. They have seen and worked with the good, the bad, and the ugly. In this book, they offer answers for any board and staff who struggle to meet both the internal and external challenges that confront boards. They can do this with aplomb because of their own personal maturity and their own experiences in dealing productively with people of all types to bring them to a point of common focus and a shared vision for the organizations they govern.

Good Governance Is a Choice lays out the values-based system they have successfully used across America and internationally to help boards, their

CEOs, and senior staff develop an understanding of, and capacity for, excellent governance and organizational performance. Effectively implementing Coherent Governance will achieve what Randy and Linda promise: "systemic, systematic, and sustainable good governance, unerringly focused on the results for clients these organizations exist to serve."

For school districts, this is the answer to disparate reform efforts that usually fail to address the pivotal role of governance in school reform. Coherent Governance focuses boards on their role as trustees of the school districts they lead on behalf of the communities they serve. This board focus is centered on student achievement and how effective the school district is in producing results defined by the board.

Performance expectations and the evaluation of the superintendent are clarified—once and for all. We know that among the more than 15,000 school districts across America, one of the major reasons for superintendent turnover is the dysfunctional relationships that develop between them and their boards.

In my opinion, this exodus must stop. It can, with strong, sustainable leadership by the board, working collaboratively with the superintendent. The governing model described in this book, Coherent Governance, provides a logical and no-nonsense, value-centered map for clarity of expectations and rigorous monitoring of the CEO and organizational performance.

The concept of teamwork defined in this book is dramatically different from the traditional understanding of that term, but it makes perfect sense as a means to establish clarity and unambiguous role expectations for both boards and their CEOs.

Good Governance Is a Choice demonstrates how governing boards can grow into successful, cooperative bodies that truly lead the organizations for which they are responsible, whether those boards govern public entities, nonprofit, or for-profit organizations.

This book is well written and is crammed full of lessons that will offer new insights for anyone who wants to improve the performance of the board on which he or she serves.

You will discover that truly, good governance is *your* choice!

Thomas A. Shannon
Attorney at Law and
Executive Director Emeritus
National School Boards Association

Preface

God must love boards. The evidence is in the existence of millions of them in the United States alone, multiplied many times over worldwide.

These millions of boards, and the well-intentioned individuals who serve on them, all are trying to contribute to the betterment of something: public schools, universities, credit unions, banks, youth clubs, associations, civic clubs, charities, foundations, insurance pools, country clubs, and music guilds. You name it; there is a board governing it—or trying to!

Despite the inherent worth of boards, for every one board that works well, there are scores of others that don't. Board members themselves far too frequently leave their positions on boards believing their valuable time has been wasted dealing not with substantive issues, but with administrative and trivial matters that should have been handled by staff.

To be brutally honest, many board members simply don't know what their jobs are. They busy themselves doing things, many times the wrong things, which results in frustration shared by everyone associated with the organization.

But it is equally important to recognize that in many instances, these frustrations are due to board members finding themselves entrenched in a governing system (we use that term loosely) so inherently inadequate that failure was unavoidable.

These facts served as our motivation for this book. It is our belief that boards have choices: they can choose to do their work the way they always have done it, whether it makes sense or not; or they can back away from their own traditions and customs and judge with fresh eyes whether what they are doing is coherent. Boards do have within their span of control the ability to change their governing culture, if they have the will to do so.

Most of our adult lives have been spent working with boards as their advocates, governance trainers, coaches, and consultants. Our specialty niche is public and nonprofit boards, and more specifically public school boards. We believe the world of public school boards to be one of the most challenging environments in which to govern well and to lead organizational change. If meaningful change can occur and be sustained here, it can succeed in any organization.

Our conclusion from more than sixty combined years' experience with governing boards is that, while differences certainly do exist between and among types of governing boards, for the most part, a board is a board. School boards, city councils, foundation boards, and hospital boards deal with different issues related to their respective industries, but all struggle with issues of board-CEO role clarity, interpersonal issues among board members, defining what success looks like for their respective organizations, and monitoring organizational performance. In our experience, there are many more similarities than differences among the many types of public and nonprofit boards.

This book includes chapters that discuss our own Coherent Governance® model and its various components. It is intended to provide for readers a broad overview of Coherent Governance, which we consider to be the single best "operating system" to enable boards to function at their highest level of effectiveness. Understanding the model and how it works prepares readers to critically assess the practicality and effectiveness of their boards' current method of doing business and whether it makes sense.

We examine some factors that prevent boards from performing at their highest level of efficiency and effectiveness, consider some of the characteristics of high-performing boards and the principles on which they base their performance, and take an in-depth look at Coherent Governance as a governing model.

At the end of each chapter we include a few Questions for Thought, which we hope will lead not only to introspection by the reader, but also by other members of the entire board on which the reader serves.

Readers will note similarities between Coherent Governance® and John Carver's Policy Governance® model. Both authors have been trained by John Carver in his model and are graduates of his Policy Governance Academy. We used that model with our clients for a number of years, with some success.

Coherent Governance features some important differences, especially in the Operational Expectations/Executive Limitations area. These differences will become more apparent to the reader in chapter 6.

We thank our many clients whose work has given us a vast supply of examples from which to draw—some good, some not. Many of their real-life experiences are discussed in the book, but we have chosen not to identify many of them by name or organization.

Coherent Governance is a model that will work with any board of any type. We want readers who have any kind of board experience to be able to relate to the content and the examples we use. But readers will note very quickly that many of our examples come from the world of school boards and public education. That choice was deliberate, for two very good reasons.

First, a large segment of our client base is composed of public school boards, and thus the supply of examples is greater. We do try to balance school board examples with others from different types of nonprofit organizations.

Second, and perhaps more important, virtually every reader is familiar with public schools and, to some extent, how they operate. All of us have a direct connection with public schools, either as a former student, as a parent of a student, or if nothing else, an "owner," one who pays for the services they provide. All of us can relate to the issues these important public institutions face.

Throughout this book, we refer to the chief administrative officer as the CEO. If your organization uses the labels "superintendent" or "executive director" or other similar title, consider the titles interchangeable.

Readers also will note that this is not an oversized book. It could have been much larger. Our goal, however, was to say what we had to say in as few words as possible. We want people to read it, all of it. We think most readers appreciate the value of word efficiency.

Finally, we want to sincerely acknowledge the millions of citizens who volunteer their time and energies to make life better for those served by our public and nonprofit organizations. Their personal sacrifices are nothing short of amazing. Many spend vast sums of their personal wealth to campaign for a public office that pays little or nothing, then devote enormous personal time to the task and still encounter constant criticism when the organizations they serve fail to meet someone's expectations. Yet they continue to serve.

It is our hope that this book will stimulate readers to examine their own board experiences and critically assess whether those boards' performance is coherent. It is our further hope that readers who serve on boards of any type will understand that good governance really is a choice available to every board, and that improved governing performance can be achieved if the board has the will to take the venture.

1

Why Don't Boards Perform Better?

A number of years ago, we conducted "exit interviews" with a number of retiring school board members. We asked them: "During your four (or eight or more) years of service to your community's schools, were you able to make the differences you hoped when you began your service?"

The overwhelming response was no.

We probed: "What prevented you from achieving all you had envisioned? What were the obstacles you encountered?"

Some of the responses were predictable: state and federal mandates, shortage of resources, union issues, and a few others. But what struck us was the number of times we heard responses indicating that the board's own internal operating systems and processes did not allow the board to do important work. Time was spent approving administrative recommendations, usually about operational issues, many times dealing with decisions that had been made long before the meeting. The board's meetings were more public ceremonies than occasions to get work done.

Precious little time was spent on "kid issues," and much time was spent on trivial operational matters. The board did not control its own agenda, but rather dealt with whatever matters the administration-created agenda asked it to do.

The real tragedy in all this is that these boards had within their own control the ability to change these limiting conditions, but neglected to do so. They yielded to the pressure of tradition and custom, and simply did what they did because that's what they had always done.

These boards failed to recognize that good governance is a choice that they themselves could make. They did make a choice, however. They decided to succumb to the inertia that bound them to a role of mediocrity. In so doing, they joined thousands, maybe millions, of other boards that, at best, are merely tolerated by the organizations they purport to lead.

These boards rely on no coherent system to get meaningful work done. They have no governing focus. They are captive to their own lack of vision for what could be.

These board members' responses reinforced our own observations over the years about the inability of boards in general to overcome their own impediments to good governance. Based on our own experiences, we offer the following factors as just a few of the self-imposed obstacles that prevent boards from performing at the high level they are capable of.

OBSTACLE 1: MISUNDERSTANDING OF THE BOARD'S JOB
Ask any group of board members what they consider to be their primary responsibility and area of focus. You may get a smattering of different responses, but the dominant answer will be policy. Instinctively, most people will agree that boards do policy. That idea is one most people have become accustomed to believing, whether they routinely observe it or not.

Now, if you are a member of a board, try this exercise: mentally reconstruct your last board meeting agenda. How many policy-level decisions did the board make? How many issues on the agenda were presented within the context of an existing board policy? What percentage of the board meeting time was devoted to policy-level discussions? These may be questions you would rather not answer, unless your board is among the few that have transformed themselves with some coherent system of governance.

In truth, most boards spend virtually no time on policy-level discussions or decisions. In fact, it could be argued that in many instances, boards and their CEOs almost have reversed roles: many boards spend almost as much time on operational matters as the CEO does, and the CEO, in creating policy drafts for the board to consider, may spend more time on policy than the board does.

Instead of resolving issues and providing organizational leadership at the policy level, most boards deal with lower-level issues one at a time, usually in a reactionary mode. Something happens, and the board senses the need to "do something."

Over the course of a few years, these boards probably make the same or very similar decisions over and over, never realizing that they could have developed a single broad policy that addresses the board's values about such matters and allowed that one policy to guide related staff decisions without further board action.

It isn't that boards resist doing their work at the policy level; rather, boards rarely take the time to consider exactly what working at the policy level actually looks like in real life.

As we will see later in this book, there are coherent ways for the board truly to operate at the policy level—and still maintain full control of the organization for which it is responsible.

OBSTACLE 2: JOB CONFUSION, VARIATION 2

Some boards believe it to be the role of the board to "manage the manager." This role perception can manifest itself in several ways, but one stands out.

The board may believe that it must "check up on" the CEO and staff at every opportunity in order to assure itself that executive decisions are being made the way the board wants them made, or to "prevent things from falling through the cracks." These boards may feel the need to appoint committees to "help" the staff with specified areas of decision making, usually in such operational areas as personnel, finance, facilities, and even curriculum (if a school board).

Think about this for a moment: boards hire the best and most capable CEOs they can find, declare the board's belief in the CEO's abilities by giving them the job, then demonstrate such lack of confidence that they ask committees, in most instances composed of laymen, to oversee staff work or help staff make decisions that are theirs to make.

Most CEOs are big boys and girls, very capable of making some very important decisions without the help of the board or a committee. The board is obligated to set the parameters for delegated decision making, as we will see in chapter 5. But if a board cannot trust the CEO in whom it expressed confidence when it made the choice to hire him or her, then perhaps that choice should be reexamined.

OBSTACLE 3: LACK OF AN EFFECTIVE OPERATING SYSTEM

Whether you are a Windows person or a Mac person, you understand the importance of a good operating system. Without it, your computer is an expensive piece of hardware that will do nothing other than fill up desk space, never helping you get work done.

Most boards seem not to realize this fact when it comes to their own work. They have no defined way to do their jobs. Members show up for meetings, follow a scripted agenda usually prepared by someone else and over which they have little control, and deal with whatever issues the agenda asks them to consider—whether those issues properly belong to the board or not.

It is not unusual for boards to have no written job description or other policy statements defining how they will conduct their business. It is rare when a board has an annual work plan that outlines what issues it will deal with during the course of the next twelve months. Although most boards realize that they are responsible for the organization's success, both outcomes and operations, few have any sensible way of assessing organizational performance.

These are examples of boards trying to get work done without a defined, well-crafted process for doing it. They are working hard, but usually accomplishing little. They have no "system" for governing, but rather do what they do because of tradition or custom. In most cases, members have not stepped away from the rote, routine work the board does to ask: *Why? Why does the board do what it does, and why does it do it that way? Are there better, more productive ways we could be spending our time?*

OBSTACLE 4: LACK OF ROLE CLARITY

In our observation, one of the most nagging challenges facing boards and their CEOs over the years has been lack of role clarity and separation of responsibilities between the board and the CEO. And considering the way many boards and CEOs interact with each other as they make decisions, this should not be surprising.

The traditional decision-making process consists of the CEO's developing and submitting to the board recommendations for the board to either approve or not. These recommendations, for the most part, are operational in nature. We call this exchange the "Mother-may-I" game: the CEO is asking the board's permission to do his job, and only if the board blesses the proposed action may it be taken.

This has become a very comfortable way for many boards and their CEOs to make decisions. From the board's standpoint, it feels powerful to be placed in the position of helping make so many important operational decisions. It offers board members the opportunity to scrutinize the CEO's and staff's decision making, and even second-guess those decisions, if so inclined.

Boards tend to feel that they are "in touch" with the operational organization through this approval role. And for the skittish CEO, what could be more comforting than to have the board on record as supporting operational decisions, just in case one of them fails to work?

Ah, but therein lies the problem: what if one of them fails to work? Who is responsible for the poor decision—the CEO who recommended it, or the board that approved it?

On a broad scale, the question is, who is accountable for decisions if both the board and the CEO share in making them? At best, we must agree that accountability is confused when decisions are made this way.

As we have worked with boards and CEOs over the years to help repair damaged relationships, it has become increasingly clear to us that as a rule, problems in the relationship generally start with role confusion. It should surprise no one that roles become confused if both the board and the CEO participate in making the very same decisions. Sooner or later, this duality will cause the relationship to degenerate.

Some people believe that "good teamwork" requires that the board and CEO work hand-in-glove to jointly reach decisions. This certainly is true, but only to a point: good teamwork is collaboration, but it does not require both parties to share in making the same decisions.

Consider an offensive football team, which has a quarterback, several offensive linemen, a running back, a blocking back, wide receivers, and a tight end or two. Each position has very well defined responsibilities, and the players who occupy each position have special skills that serve them well in their respective assignments. The team does not huddle and make a group decision about which play to run.

In our view, good teamwork requires both the board and the CEO to understand very well what their jobs are, what their specific assignments are, and who is accountable for what. Then each must respect the decisions of the other, as long as those decisions are within the preapproved "game plan," in this case the board's policies.

As with any team, when all the players perform their assigned roles well, success usually comes. When they begin arguing about which play to run, or who should decide what, or start second-guessing the decisions properly made by the party who owns the responsibility for the decision, the fabric of the team begins to disintegrate.

This recommendation-approval process for decision making has other pitfalls to consider. What happens if the board and CEO agree to take a specific course of action that later proves in need of change? If the board approved a course of action, that action cannot be changed without additional board action. Administrative agility is lost in such a cumbersome process.

As we shall see in chapter 6, there is a better way for boards to guide decision making at the operational level, without relinquishing control of those decisions and without managing the manager.

OBSTACLE 5: FAILURE TO EFFECTIVELY MANAGE THE BOARD'S OWN PERFORMANCE

Even with a sound operating system, clear understanding of roles and job responsibility, some boards fail to live up to their promise due to the poor performance of individual members. Most board members are well intentioned and highly motivated to contribute to the overall effectiveness of the entire board. However, as we all have seen, there are exceptions.

Some individual members are not interested in any type of teamwork with their colleagues. They are driven by different agendas, and no process, system, or norm will force them to work effectively with other members of the board for the common good of the board and the organization.

There are viable solutions for this problem, which we will address in chapter 4. Suffice it to say here that if the board's performance is being hindered by the performance of an individual member, it is the board's responsibility to deal with the problem by whatever means it can.

OBSTACLE 6: LACK OF LONG-TERM VISION
FOR THE ORGANIZATION AND THE BOARD

Boards tend to have a short-term focus, usually based on the most recent crisis to confront it or the organization. If there is no crisis or extraordinary concern on the board's radar screen, the board tends to "hunker down" and take the position that things are just fine, thank you, and there is no good reason to rock the boat.

As experienced board members, especially those who serve on public boards, fully understand, the interval between crises really is very short. Crises cannot be avoided; they can only be managed. If boards see themselves as being nothing more than managers of crises, their vision for themselves and for the organizations they govern will always be short.

If one looks at volunteer board service pragmatically, one will conclude that all board members are transient by nature. That may sound a bit basic, but the fact is that boards and their members change. The short period of time members spend on a governing board is time out of their lives that should count for something. It is possible for legacies to be left for those who follow, but only if members can forge some shared vision about what the organizations for which they are responsible should be like at some point in the future.

The challenge for all board members while they are in service to the organization is to create something bigger than themselves, and leave that as a legacy of excellence for those who follow.

SUMMARY

Boards throughout the ages have found creative ways to limit their own effectiveness. We have listed just some of those examples, including misunderstanding of the job of the board, role confusion between the board and the CEO, the absence of an effective operating system for the board to do its work, the negative influence of individual members who distract the board and staff, and short-term vision by the board. There are many more.

In the chapters that follow, we will define what a high-performing board looks like and discuss an operating system that can help boards find answers to the challenge to provide creative leadership to the organizations for which they are responsible.

QUESTIONS FOR THOUGHT

1 If you serve on a board, does your board demonstrate any of these performance-inhibiting characteristics? Which ones?
2. Has the board recognized the problems created by any of these behaviors?
3. If so, has the board taken any steps to improve its performance?

What Does a High-Performing Board Look Like?

We, as all consultants, have a bag of tricks we use with client boards to help them critically look at themselves and judge whether their performance is what they want it to be. One of those tricks in our bag is this one.

We ask members if they ever have observed a board of any type, and made the decision, by some process, that the board either was a "good board" or a "bad board." Then we ask them to list on a sheet of paper the criteria they used to reach that judgment. In other words, what behaviors did they see or expect to see that would qualify a board to be considered "good"?

After the individuals list their responses, we compile them and use the compilation as a standard against which to assess the board's own performance.

Over the years, we have observed a strong similarity among the responses of individual board members about what they themselves believe constitutes a "good"—or high-performing—board. We share with you here the common characteristics contributed by those board members.

1: HIGH-PERFORMING BOARDS KNOW WHAT THEIR JOB IS

In fact, most of our client boards have a policy called "Board Job Description," which clearly defines in writing what the members of the board believe they are there to do. This job description drives the content of board meeting agendas because the meeting is where the board generally does whatever it does.

If the board determines that it needs the assistance of a committee, the legitimacy of the committee is based upon whether it supports the board's job description. Logically, any board committee should help the board do its job, not help the CEO do the CEO's job.

If the board is not very clear about what its job is, it is very likely that the board will find itself doing someone else's job.

2: HIGH-PERFORMING BOARDS FUNCTION AT THE LEVEL OF POLICY

This means that the board has found ways to guide the CEO and the organization at a high, broad level, and has delegated to staff the detailed decision making associated with day-to-day operations of the organization. Policy-level decision making means controlling decisions without making them, relying on broad, well-conceived policies to convey board expectations to staff about related smaller issues.

It's not unlike being the parents of a teenager: we convey expectations about acceptable behavior and monitor actual behaviors against those expectations, realizing that it isn't good practice to make decisions for them—even if we could!

3: HIGH-PERFORMING BOARDS CREATE THEIR OWN GOVERNING CULTURE

Actually, they not only create their own culture, but they also assess themselves against their agreed-upon performance standards. Good boards know the behaviors expected of them, and they regularly monitor their own performance to assure that those behaviors are being practiced. Ideally, expected performance standards are created by the board and recorded as board policy.

At least annually, the board does a complete self-assessment, consisting of comparison of actual board performance and behavior against the standards the board set in policy. Corrective action plans to close the gaps between performance and the standard must be a component of the exercise.

4: HIGH-PERFORMING BOARDS FOLLOW THE RULES

It is one thing to set performance standards for the board, and sometimes quite another to actually comply with those rules. The board expects staff to faithfully observe and comply with all policies governing organizational behavior, but when members of the board are confronted with a situation in which expedience runs headlong into one of the board's own policies governing member or board commitments, sometimes the board or its members are tempted to come down on the side of expedience.

This isn't playing fair, nor is it playing by the rules. Staff and outsiders expect consistent and predictable behavior by organizations, including their governing boards. If rules aren't important and are not going to be observed, then maybe they should not be adopted at all.

5: HIGH-PERFORMING BOARDS PLAN THEIR OWN WORK

We have discovered something about boards: they generally will do whatever work the agenda asks them to do.

In more instances than some might imagine, it is the CEO who usually prepares the proposed board meeting agenda, and (maybe) sends it to the board president for a quick look before it goes to the board as the meeting's work plan. This is not critical of CEOs, who, after all, usually will try to do whatever the board expects them to do or lead the board to conduct its business consistent with the CEO's vision of appropriate board work.

For a CEO to be responsible for determining the work of the board simply makes no sense. We all agree that there are matters that the CEO legitimately should be free to present to the board, and therefore the CEO must have some role in creating the proposed agenda. But it is the *board's* meeting, and *the board itself should be responsible for what goes on the agenda.* The best way for the board to plan its own work is to develop an annual work plan, which will drive the content of board meeting agendas. These plans are updated each year when the board conducts its annual planning retreat.

6: HIGH-PERFORMING BOARDS HAVE A LONG-TERM VISION

That vision must exist for both the organization and for the board itself. It has been said that if a person does not know where he is going, any road will get him there. It's the same for organizations. We believe the board, not the CEO or staff, should own the vision for where the organization is headed, and assure that systems are in place to realize that long-term vision.

Too many times we have seen boards seek a CEO with "vision." Let us acknowledge that a CEO being a visionary leader is far better than not, but if the CEO brings the vision with him when he comes, it usually leaves with him when he goes. On behalf of the ownership of the organization to which the board is accountable, the vision for where the organization is headed should be the board's, not the CEO's.

7: HIGH-PERFORMING BOARDS FOCUS ON OUTCOMES

It isn't unusual to find board meeting agendas consisting entirely of matters related to organizational processes and operational functions, with no attention whatsoever to whether the organization is succeeding in achieving its mission or any of its client-centered goals.

High-performing boards develop client-centered outcomes the organization is expected to achieve (we call them Results policies), and each meeting is dominated by discussions about those outcomes: whether adequate progress is being made toward their achievement; whether all classes of customers are being served as expected; whether resources are being applied in reasonable proportions to reach success.

Boards not defined as high performing are content dealing with the "stuff" of organizational activity; high-performing boards realize that isn't where the action really is.

8: HIGH-PERFORMING BOARDS UNDERSTAND THE SEPARATION OF RESPONSIBILITY BETWEEN THE BOARD AND THE CEO

There is, somewhere, a very clear line dividing the responsibilities of these two entities. It varies somewhat from board to board, but for any specific board, that line is there. It is up to the board to decide where the line is drawn.

In chapter 6, we discuss a technique that we believe separates the responsibilities of the board and CEO in such a way that never should there be confusion about whose job it is to do what.

9: MEMBERS OF HIGH-PERFORMING BOARDS DEAL CONSISTENTLY AND FAIRLY WITH EACH OTHER AND WITH THEIR CEO

Boards are made up of individuals, and this frequently is where the most difficult issues arise. Some members seem to have little interest in working in a collegial manner with other members or with the CEO. Instead, they seem to thrive on controversy; when it isn't there naturally, they tend to create it.

When a board finds itself with a member who consistently and egregiously places himself outside the group by such behaviors, the board has an obligation to deal with the issue in whatever way it can. We offer some suggestions later in this book.

10: HIGH-PERFORMING BOARDS OPERATE EFFICIENTLY

We frequently are asked, "How long should a board meeting last?" There really isn't a ready answer to the question. But the fact that it is being asked probably means that board meetings for the board on which the member serves are too lengthy!

The more critical question is, what is the board doing when it meets? If it requires five hours to do the work the board should be doing, that isn't too long. If it requires only two hours to do something meaningless, then why meet at all?

But if there is a belief that meeting times are too long, the board can do a number of things to assure increased efficiency. Adoption of some of them will require members to do things differently, which sometimes they are unwilling to do.

We are fans of timed agenda items, even if the board needs to exceed the allotted times upon occasion. The fact that times are printed on the agenda can call attention to their being exceeded. Boards never should underestimate the power of a deadline.

From our review of hundreds, maybe thousands of agendas, we are convinced that many items typically showing up on board meeting agendas don't need to be there at all. After all, the board meeting isn't the only place or occasion when members can be informed about something. Many items that do have a logical place on the agenda could be disposed of via consent action, as opposed to talking about them all individually and taking separate action on each.

Some boards have agreed to limit the "talk time" of each member as a means to prevent domination or repetition.

The potential strategies for making meetings more efficient are unlimited, but the message here is that if meetings are perceived to be too long, the board can exercise controls and bring itself to a higher level of efficiency—if it chooses to do so. The number one efficiency strategy: focus on policy-level decisions, and stay out of operational approvals and mundane discussions about things that have little importance.

11: HIGH-PERFORMING BOARDS NEVER EMBARRASS THEMSELVES OR THE ORGANIZATION

As trustees for the owners, the board is obligated to assure acceptable performance by the organization. The challenge is to deal effectively with problems and issues, but do so without publicly criticizing the CEO or staff, as well as other members of the board.

For members of public boards especially, this can be difficult. Public boards in every state are controlled by various open meetings laws, meaning that virtually every issue they discuss and every action they take is open to the public and often recorded on camera. Boards cannot afford to allow organizational performance issues to go unchallenged.

But in doing the required work of the board, it isn't necessary to level public criticism at individuals. Most open meetings laws allow anything related to the performance of an individual to be discussed legally in a closed meeting.

It is our belief that the board should deal publicly and openly with organizational performance issues, but reserve any comments critical of individuals to a legally convened closed session.

12: HIGH-PERFORMING BOARDS ARE IN TOUCH WITH THEIR "OWNERS"

Someone owns all organizations. Sometimes the ownership is a challenge to identify, but usually it is very clear. If you are a public board of any type, you will agree that the ownership is the public itself: the citizens who are served by your organization.

Board members of any organization are there because the owners themselves are not; they have entrusted the board to lead, serve, and represent their interests. In other words, the board is the owners' "proxy."

What this means to the board is that the board must maintain some type of ongoing relationship with the owners in order to understand owners' expectations, as well as to assure that the owners understand the effectiveness and the challenges of the organization's work.

We emphasize that this is a *board* function, not an *individual board member* responsibility. At least in terms of public boards, whose members usually are elected, members may have their own network of people with whom they interact. This concept extends to the board as an entity and demands precise board strategies in order to accomplish.

Most boards don't do a very good job of meeting this expectation; they purposefully plan and connect with the owners only when something is needed in return, but usually not at any other time.

SUMMARY

High-performing boards are characterized by a number of observable behaviors. They know what their job is, and they do it efficiently. They plan their own work and perform their work at the policy level, focusing more on organizational outcomes than process.

They are responsible for their own performance; they follow their own rules and deal fairly and consistently with staff and each other. They set the vision for themselves and the organization.

They understand clearly the separation of responsibilities between their work and the work of the CEO. They are in touch with the ownership, to which they are accountable.

QUESTIONS FOR THOUGHT

1. Do you consider your board to be a high-performing board?
2. How many of these behaviors characterize your board?
3. Has your board discussed ways to improve its performance in any of the areas covered by these high-performance characteristics?

3

Governing Coherently or Incoherently?

If you serve on a board, the board has a history. The board has carved out for itself a culture, a way of doing business, that probably is based more on historical custom than on a deliberately designed plan.

Let's turn back time for a minute. Let's place you in the position of having been elected or appointed to serve as a member of the very first board empowered to govern your organization. The board is meeting for the first time and has the opportunity to decide, with a fresh set of eyes, unencumbered by any historical customs, how it will do its work. There are no policies, no bylaws, no minutes of previous meetings, no history to overcome.

How would you propose to create a governing system that would allow the board to do its work in the best possible way? What would the board's agendas look like? What would the board's work plan for the next year include? How would the board's relationship with the CEO be defined? How would the board's job be described? What would constitute a productive way for the members to interact with each other? What results is the organization expected to produce, and for whom? At what cost? What processes would the board put in place to assure effective organizational performance?

Wouldn't that be an exciting opportunity! It is easy to make the assumption that only a new board enjoys such a luxury. But in fact, every board can exercise these options, if it is willing to suspend its disbelief and free itself from the binds of historical customs that, in many instances, inhibit good governance.

Boards tend to be captives of inertia: things are as they are because they always have been that way. Board meetings are more ceremonial events than productive business meetings because the board—and perhaps its onlookers— has come to expect such performances.

Various reports show up on board meeting agendas, whether the board wants or needs the information or not, because custom calls for it. Boards approve administrative recommendations about operational issues because that has become the rote way of managing the organization, not because the board has carefully decided which decisions it chooses to reserve for itself and which it wishes to delegate—and assign accountability for.

THE NEED FOR AN OPERATING SYSTEM

We discussed in chapter 1 the need for an effective operating system to enable the board to do its work in some coherent fashion. If the board has an operating system, but a poorly designed one, it can be a greater liability than an asset.

Boards seem not to realize these facts. In our experience, most boards have no defined operating system at all. They have never deliberately, consciously decided how the board should go about the task of governing the organization. They do things, to be sure, usually based on habit and history, not on the basis of a well-designed system for good governance.

These boards are governing incoherently. They have no system or process in place that provides the framework for sound governance. And because there is no established framework, they more often than not stay very busy doing the wrong things. Their members are frustrated that their hard work doesn't seem to be having much positive impact on the organization.

In fact, all that hard work can be greeted with disdain from the staff, who see the board encroaching into their work more than providing policy-level leadership to guide the organization. Next come strained relationships, which can lead to cultural disintegration at every level.

Just what do we mean by an "operating system" for boards? First, this is what we do not mean: we do not advocate for some Old Testament–style, rigid governing system that binds boards to the point that they can achieve no meaningful work. We have seen boards become enslaved to a rigid, inflexible system so confining that the board becomes a captive to its own self-imposed governing model.

Models are just that: models. They are not the ends themselves, but rather they are means to the end: good governance. Some boards adopt a governing model, then, without proper understanding of how to use it, allow it to limit their own performance in ways that are (that word again) incoherent. Governing models should limit bad board behavior; they should not limit the board's ability to do its job.

In our view, policy-based models are superior to others for a number of reasons. The board, at least in theory, is expected to operate at the policy level. Policy decisions by their nature carry more weight than other types of decisions, and their reach is farther and wider.

As you will see in subsequent chapters, we advocate for an operating system that is expressed entirely in board policy, and that binds the board to certain behaviors and commitments just as firmly as other parts bind the staff.

Boards, of any type, must have a certain level of discipline in order to add value to the organizations they govern. They can't simply make up the rules as they go, inconsistently doing whatever "feels" right at the time. They can't thoughtlessly go through the motions of governing by continuing to do what they did five years ago, whether it makes sense or not.

Boards occupy a position at the top of the organizational chart that demands that they govern, that they provide leadership in a way that is unique to the board, setting the standards for organizational success, establishing the parameters within which the staff is expected to work, and assigning accountability for results. The board has an obligation to lead by example.

GOVERNING COHERENTLY

Regardless of the type, size, or nature of the organization, we believe it is possible for a governing board to effectively govern the organization for which it is responsible with a set of well-crafted policies numbering not more than thirty, total. For some organizations, that may seem completely unrealistic, given the historical culture of the board and organization. Our use of board policy, however, is very different from the way most organizations use policy, especially school boards and other public boards.

We'll use school boards as the example. It is not at all uncommon to see school board policy manuals that are five inches thick, occupying one or more three-ring binders. We frequently ask school board members when they tend to use those policies. The consistent answer: when they encounter problems.

Examination of policies of this type usually establishes that most of them are there because of state or federal mandates, and that most of them are operational in nature. Most are very detailed and are intended to guide day-to-day operations and cover numerous operational contingencies.

While they may be based on good intentions, these mandated actions create role confusion by requiring board approval of operational programs and decisions, which are better made by CEOs and staff.

It is rare when we find a board member who even knows what is in those policies. After all, there may be hundreds of them, so this should not be surprising.

In truth, a governing board striving to lead an organization cannot effectively use policies of this type and volume. They can be useful to a CEO and administration, who are "on the ground" dealing with such issues. But for a governing board to rely on a policy manual (populated by hundreds of very detailed, very operationally focused, mostly mandated policies) is wishing for a level of meaningful leadership that is unlikely to be realized.

We usually suggest that policies of this type be labeled "district policies" or "operational policies," and separated entirely from the board's governing policies, which we will discuss in more detail later in this book. These operational policies become the responsibility of the CEO and staff, who are required to operate both legally and consistently with the board's broad governing policies.

Since law requires many of these policies, we recommend that they retain the "policy" label, rather than being called "regulations" or "rules." If legal mandates change or if new operational policies are required by subsequent legislative action, we suggest that the board approve what it is required to approve, but do so via consent agenda and place the new policy in the operational policy manual rather than in its governance policy manual. The board cannot live in both worlds.

COHERENT GOVERNANCE: A CONCEPTUAL FRAMEWORK

Earlier we discussed ways in which boards tend to behave incoherently as they struggle to find a meaningful way to do their work, without a defined system to guide them in that effort. We label our governing model Coherent

Governance® to reflect its basic intent: to provide the framework for coherent board focus and process.

The dictionary defines these two key words as follows: "*Govern*: to have or exercise a determining influence; to have political authority"; "*Coherent*: sticking together; marked by an orderly or logical relation of parts that affords comprehension or recognition; logically consistent."

It is indisputable that boards have determining influence and, if a public board, political authority over the organizations they govern. That is the nature of a board, a role sometimes played skillfully, at other times very awkwardly. Our objective is to offer an operating system that enables boards to perform their roles in a way that is orderly and consistent and that makes sense when viewed as a whole functional entity.

Coherent Governance is based upon a set of twelve principles that are reflected in various parts of the model. These twelve principles are not unlike the characteristics of effective boards that we discussed earlier in chapter 2. They serve as the basis for building a model that helps boards actually perform in a manner consistent with the principles.

Principle 1: The Board Serves as Trustee for the Owners

As basic as this sounds, many boards seem not to understand for whom they work. They become confused when they hear from inside and outside pressure groups, and sometimes rationalize that they are acting on behalf of the owners—when they have heard from only a single element of that ownership, one that happens to be motivated to share its opinion with the board.

If the board is serious about serving the complete ownership when it makes decisions, it is necessary to devise mechanisms for the board to interface with that ownership on a continuous basis, not just when the board wants something from the owners.

Notice that we said board, not board members. All individual members have their own networks of people with whom they interact on a regular basis. This is insufficient as a means to enable the full board to understand the expectations of the ownership. Effective engagement with the ownership requires the board to have a well-crafted communication plan for itself.

This does not negate the importance of the CEO's or the operational organization's having a plan for communicating, but it does underscore the fact that the board, as trustee for the ownership, has a different role to play in communicating with those owners.

Principle 2: The Board Knows What Its Job Is, and It Is Responsible for Its Own Performance

One of the most important policies in the Coherent Governance model is the one that defines the board's job. Without a job description, the board will do whatever feels right at the time.

The absence of a well-crafted job description is one of the primary reasons for such rampant role confusion that exists in many organizations, especially public organizations. Once the board creates a job description, it should drive meeting agendas—which is where most board work is done. In addition, it should help draw the line between legitimate board committees—which should serve the work of the board—and other committees that assist the work of the CEO.

Defining the work and actually doing it are two separate issues. Once the board has defined its job, it then must assume responsibility for doing that job well. Monitoring board performance is not the CEO's job. The task of monitoring board performance belongs to the board itself.

Principle 3: The Board Plans Its Own Work and Focuses on Governance Matters

We have discussed in earlier chapters the fact that board meeting agendas typically are prepared by the CEO or staff and are handed to the board, which usually follows the script during meetings. The board should recognize that meetings are theirs, not the CEO's. CEOs have issues that must be submitted to the board at times, and therefore should have a hand in deciding some of the matters that appear on the agenda.

But the board should have an annual work plan, consisting of all the matters it chooses to focus on during the year. This annual work plan then in turn drives the agendas for each meeting. The dominant concern of the board should be whether the organization is achieving reasonable progress toward meeting defined organizational outcomes, not on the operational issues that should be delegated to the CEO and staff.

Principle 4: The Board Is Active but Not Intrusive

Passive boards that do little other than what they are coached to do add little value to the organization. Overactive boards that dig into the daily operations of the organization can be distractions, or even destructive impediments for the organization they are trying to help.

Boards really can be active, contributing members of the organization's leadership without interfering in its day-to-day operations. The Coherent Governance model was built as a means to help boards do that.

Principle 5: The Board Acts as a Unit

Unanimous decisions always are desirable, but not always possible. That's OK. When unanimity cannot be achieved, business must go on. The board acts as a unit, not as a collection of individuals. A close majority vote of the board is just as binding as a unanimous one.

CEOs and staff members sometimes feel it is their obligation to satisfy each individual member of the board, and in making this attempt they succumb to the temptation to do things based on nothing more than what they heard one member say. Bad practice. Direction is given when the board votes, and not until.

Principle 6: The Board Rigorously Monitors Both the Organization's and Its Own Performance

Boards must delegate significant authority to CEOs and staff to make good things happen for the organization, but they cannot safely do so without some corresponding performance accountability process.

This means that every operational function should be monitored regularly, without delaying operational reviews until something bad happens. Even more importantly, the board must effectively monitor whether the organization is aligned and producing the outcomes the board has said it should. Monitoring organizational performance should be a significant component of the board's job description, and it should constitute a major part of every board meeting.

In addition, good boards monitor their own performance as rigorously as they monitor organizational performance. Self-monitoring should occur after each meeting through a debriefing process, and more thoroughly at least once each year in a board retreat.

Principle 7: The Board Controls Organizational Operation Through Policy, not Through Approvals

Traditionally, boards have controlled operational decisions through either approving or not approving administrative recommendations. There are ways that boards can control such decisions without helping the CEO make them via this approval process. They can do so through well-crafted policy, as we will discuss in chapter 6.

Principle 8: The Board Owns the Vision for the Organization

As the trustee for the owners, it is the board's duty to decide what the organization should look like and achieve. CEOs and other important players can contribute to that vision, but it is the board's responsibility to translate owner expectations into statements of aspiration that can create a meaningful future for the organization.

Principle 9: He Who Makes the Decision Is Accountable For It

We wrote earlier in a number of places about the confused accountability that results from the board's approval of administrative recommendations—and we will talk more about it throughout this book. This principle simply states that those who make decisions must assume the accountability that flows from the actions they take. This accountability cannot be shifted to anyone who did not make the decision.

**Principle 10: The Performance of the Organization
and the Performance of the CEO Are Identical**

This is a significant concept, one with which some CEOs may not be completely comfortable. The CEO should be granted significant authority to do the job for which he or she has been hired. In the Coherent Governance model, this means operating the organization in a manner consistent with the board's operational policy values, and making reasonable progress toward achieving the board's defined outcomes for clients.

The CEO's and the organization's performance are monitored and evaluated simultaneously.

**Principle 11: The Board Delegates Authority
to the CEO to Do the Job, but Within Stated Parameters**

It is true that the CEO has greater authority in the Coherent Governance model than many do in more traditional governance environments. However, this authority is not unlimited; the board always controls the extent of delegated authority and establishes the limits through policy.

**Principle 12: The CEO Is Accountable for
Decisions Within the Area of Delegated Authority**

With authority comes accountability. This principle is a counterbalance to Principle 11. The two work in tandem.

THE COHERENT GOVERNANCE FRAMEWORK

Coherent Governance is a governing model composed of four separate, but interrelated, types of policies. In the chapters that follow, we will discuss each of these policy types in greater detail. For now, these are the four types of policies and their general purpose:

1. *Governance Culture.* GC policies, usually about ten or so in number, combine to create an overall culture of good board performance. The policies challenge the board to create, very carefully and deliberately, a desired culture that will become the standard for board and board member performance.
2. *Board-CEO Relationship.* BCR policies, typically five in number, define the authority delegated by the board to the CEO and the accountability of the CEO for organizational results and overall performance.
3. *Operational Expectations.* OE policies express the board's values about all parts of operational activity. They guide CEO and staff decision making by specifying the actions and conditions the board expects to exist as well as those the board will not permit. Typically, a board may have from eight to twelve OE policies.
4. *Results.* R policies convey the board's expectations about organizational outcomes the board demands on behalf of the organization's owners and clients.

Properly conceived and constructed, the thirty or so policies in these four areas will give the board all the tools it needs to properly create its own culture, specify expected outcomes for the people served by the organization, guide and control the organization's actions at the operations level, and effectively delegate operational decisions and hold staff accountable for results. We believe these are the only viable reasons for a board to exist.

SUMMARY

All boards have a culture; in most instances, it is due not to design, but to tradition. Most boards do not have a functional operating system for getting their work done, but instead rely on custom and tradition, or "seat-of-the-pants" operational processes. In the public sector at least, most board policy manuals are large and cumbersome, based more on legal requirements about operational matters than on the board's own values about the organization. Boards effectively can govern a complex organization with a few very broad, well-conceived, and well-crafted governing policies.

QUESTIONS FOR THOUGHT

1. If you had the opportunity to create a new governing culture for your board, as presented at the beginning of this chapter, how would your creation compare with the reality of the way your board now operates?
2. Has your board ever had a discussion about the way it does its work and, equally important, the actual type of work the board does?
3. How many policies does your board now have? Do you know their content?

4

Constructing the Board's Own Governing Culture

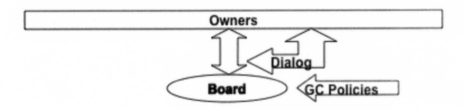

Every board has a culture. In most instances, we aren't quite sure how it got to be what it is. Boards tend to do what they do, and members tend to behave the way they do, because of tradition and custom. These traditions and customs usually evolve over the years and become institutionalized because of inertia. This doesn't mean that they all are bad or unproductive. However, in most cases the culture that exists is not based on careful planning or forethought— or even a stated goal of excellence.

In chapter 3 we presented the intriguing thought that a board should free itself from tradition and custom and redesign its own governing culture as if it were meeting for the very first time. We should acknowledge that in many instances, the board's old ways of doing business might be fine. There is nothing inherently wrong with customs and traditions, unless a board becomes so blinded by them that it cannot see the potential for doing things differently and better.

In this chapter, we discuss how boards may re-create themselves, building in a very careful, deliberate way a governing culture that makes sense, hopefully even qualifying as a legacy the board will be proud to leave for those who follow.

From observation, we have learned that competent people and competent boards do not necessarily travel together. We have worked with boards whose members included federal judges, CEOs, doctors, attorneys, business consultants, and other such professional types, who so disliked each other they were unable even to look at each other when they spoke. In some instances, high-powered individuals, each of them leaders in their own right, simply cannot function productively as members of a group.

One of the problems is that board members generally don't enjoy the luxury of selecting their colleagues, who usually are chosen by someone else: a membership, the public, shareholders, or some other larger ownership group. But here they all are, thrust together at the same board table, all with their individual ideas and concepts about how to do the job of leading and guiding the organization.

As individuals, each member may be qualified in some way as a leader, but when competing and conflicting ideas, styles, and preferences are thrown into the mix, the group is unable to govern as a unit, given all the tenacious polarity of thought and ideas.

So just how does a group of capable individuals forge some type of operating system that will allow it to get past the obstacles of individual styles, differences, and preferences—even dislike of other members?

Let us acknowledge here that we have worked with a few boards whose individual makeup was such that no solution was workable. Some individual members have no interest in anything resembling effective group performance, preferring instead to "go it alone" and do their own thing.

Especially in the public arena, we occasionally find elected board members who feel it appropriate to assert their First Amendment rights, regardless of the impact the exercise of those rights might have on the board and the organization. These members have not accepted the idea that not all rights must be exercised at all times, without regard for the consequences of such irresponsible action.

Nor have they learned that the group is more than the sum of its parts, and that the board actually is more important than its individual members.

In order for any system of governance to effectively guide a board to a high level of performance, the members of the board must recognize the need to subordinate some individual rights and preferences for the benefit of the governing body and organization.

CREATING A GOVERNANCE CULTURE

Absent internal obstacles of this type, boards willing to critically examine their role and purpose and the ways they do their work can rebuild themselves through a process that allows the members to create a governance culture that makes sense to them. As discussed earlier, our Coherent Governance model is composed of four types of policies, the first of which, Governance Culture (GC), provides the vehicle for the board to thoughtfully accomplish this task.

GC policies recognize that the board, regardless of the type of organization it governs, is accountable to an ownership. In fact, it is reasonable to think of the board as the owners' proxy. The board is at the board table because the ownership itself is not; it has empowered a small group of people to act on its behalf in leading and guiding the organization.

Thus it is critically important for any board first to define, very clearly, who its ownership is. Someone owns every organization. In most cases, identification of that ownership is a fairly easy decision to make. We probably would agree that the public at large owns a school district—even though the direct client group usually is composed of the children of about 20 percent of that ownership.

That same group of citizens probably owns a city government, but in this case the owners and the clients are the same. A voluntary membership organization may belong to that membership, but upon closer examination, the organization could have a larger purpose that could cause the definition of ownership to be somewhat broader than the membership itself.

One of our clients is a nonprofit organization in Seattle that provides elder-care services for Japanese Americans. The organization has no members. Its board of directors is self-perpetuating, meaning that the board itself appoints or reappoints members. Most of the organization's financial support comes from grants and projects, in addition to fees paid by clients themselves.

The ownership of this organization is not as evident as it would be if it had a defined membership or if members of the board were elected by someone.

The board has decided that "the Japanese community of Greater Seattle" owns it.

The ownership, however defined by the board, is the entity to which the board is accountable. We suggest that boards think of their obligation to their ownership as being a combination of leading, serving, and representing. To consider the board's role as one of nothing more than representing is to simplify and limit the role to the point of making the board meaningless. If the only role a board plays is one of representation, the board may not be needed at all; a good computer program could allow the ownership itself to guide the organization without the board's help.

Leading and serving an ownership take on added challenge and meaning for the board. There are times when the three roles suggested here come into conflict with each other.

If the members of the board are publicly elected, they may hear one direction being advocated by the public, while knowing that in order to serve that public's long-term interests in the best possible way, a different course of action is called for. No governing model will take away the difficulty of a board's managing these inevitable conflicts, but it is important to recognize the reality of them, to anticipate them, and to make conscious decisions about how best to deal with them when they occur.

Once the ownership has been defined, the board's next step is to carve out for itself a set of governing policies that, collectively, define the overall culture the board chooses for itself. Once drafted and approved, these policies become the standard against which the board should assess its own actual performance.

As we shall see in subsequent chapters, each type of policy sets performance standards for some part of the organization, and through regular monitoring of actual performance against those standards, no part of the organization, the board included, goes without evaluation during the course of an annual cycle.

In our work with boards that choose this course of action, we prefer to begin here, in the GC quadrant. It is our belief that the board should get its own act together before it assumes the task of developing policies governing the organization.

The primary point to be made about GC policies is that they have nothing to do with any part of the organization except the board itself. In fact, the policies in this quadrant are the board's own operating system.

GOVERNANCE CULTURE POLICIES

For most boards, regardless of type of organization, the GC section is composed of nine or ten separate policies, each addressing a topic related to the behavior of the board or its members or the processes the board will use to perform its responsibilities. Boards governing certain types of organizations may determine the need for a few additional policies specifically related to the board's job in such an environment—fund-raising, for example, if members are expected to do such work.

Typically, however, most boards rely on a nucleus of GC policies covering the following topics:

GC-1: Board Purpose
Who are the owners? To whom is the board responsible? Why does the board exist? What purpose does it serve in support of the owners' interest in this organization?

GC-2: Governing Commitments
As this board and its members do their work, what commitments do they make to themselves and to the owners? What will be the board's primary focus? How will the board assess its own performance? What commitments do the members make for themselves in terms of group participation, meeting behaviors, and personal discipline?

GC-3: Board Job Description
What is the board's job? Once specified in policy, how does the work the board actually does compare with the work the policy says it should do?

GC-4: Officers' Roles
What officer positions are there? How much authority does the board convey to its president? What specific limitations are imposed on the president? What are the duties of the other officer positions?

GC-5: Board Committees
What, by definition, is a board committee? How does a board committee differ from a CEO committee? What are the board-approved committees? What is their purpose and charge? When do they report? What authority do they have over organizational resources? Who serves on them? When does the committee cease to exist?

GC-6: Annual Work Plan
What work will the board be doing for the next twelve months? Which policies will be monitored when? With which ownership groups will the board meet, and for what purpose? In what knowledge and skill areas does the board need development opportunities? What other events and actions should the board schedule on its annual work plan in order to drive regular meeting agenda content?

GC-6-E (exhibit)
The actual annual work plan, including all items listed in the policy.

GC-7: Code of Conduct
What behaviors are expected of individual members? What behaviors are not tolerated?

GC-8: Conflict of Interest
What constitutes a conflict of interest? What is expected of a member when a conflict arises?

GC-9: Addressing Member Violations
What does the board do when a member unknowingly, willfully and/or repeatedly violates one of the board's own policies? What remedies should the board consider if it is confronted by destructive maverick behavior?

As is apparent, these policy topics and their content are not specifically related to any single type of organization; every kind of board likely will find the need for some policy statement related to all of these topics. We have included later in this chapter samples of two GC policy templates (exhibits 4.1 and 4.2). Each board will prefer certain changes, deletions, or additions, but the templates provide a sound starting place for each board's own values to be incorporated.

SUMMARY
Boards can create their own governing culture, but it is necessary to let go of some past practices and customs. Competent people don't always create competent boards. Individuals must at times subordinate their own personal interests, rights, and preferences for the benefit of the board itself in order to create a coherent board. Somebody owns every organization. The board

serves the ownership in ways that go beyond simple representation. Most boards can create a comprehensive, policy-based governing culture through the careful crafting of nine or so policies, which collectively set the expected performance standard for the board and its members.

QUESTIONS FOR THOUGHT

1. On a scale of 1 to 10, how bound to custom and tradition do you consider your board to be?
2. Who do you believe owns the organization served by your board?
3. Does your board now have a clear set of performance standards for itself and an evaluation process to assess performance against those standards?

EXHIBIT 4.1

GC-2

Policy Type: Governance Culture
Governing Commitments
The Board will govern lawfully with primary emphasis on Results for clients; encourage full exploration of diverse viewpoints; focus on governance matters rather than administrative issues; observe clear separation of Board and CEO roles; make all official decisions by formal vote of the Board; and govern with long-term vision.

2.1. *The Board will direct the organization through policy.* The Board's major focus will be on the results expected to be achieved for clients, rather than on the strategic choices made by the CEO and staff to achieve those results.

2.2. *The Board will function as a single unit.* The opinions and personal strengths of individual members will be used to the Board's best advantage, but the Board faithfully will make decisions as a group, by formal vote. No officer, individual, or committee of the Board will be permitted to limit the Board's performance or prevent the Board from fulfilling its commitments.

2.3. *The Board is responsible for its own performance, and commits itself to continuous improvement.* As a means to assure continuous improvement, the Board regularly and systematically will monitor all policies in this section and will assess the quality of each meeting by debriefing the meeting following its conclusion.

2.4. *The Board will assure that the Board and its members have the knowledge, skills, and budget support it determines to be necessary for effective governance.*

Accordingly:

a. Training will be used as necessary to orient candidates and new members, as well as to maintain and increase current member skills and knowledge, including consultative coaching and attendance at conferences and workshops;

b. External monitoring assistance will be used as necessary to enable the Board to exercise confident control over organizational performance. This includes a fiscal audit and other third-party monitoring of organizational performance;

c. Stakeholder dialog strategies will be used as needed to ensure the Board's ability to listen effectively to stakeholder viewpoints and values. This includes surveys, focus groups, opinion analyses, and dialog meeting costs.

2.5. *To ensure that the Board's business meetings are conducted with maximum effectiveness and efficiency, members will:*

a. come to meetings adequately prepared

b. speak only when recognized

c. not interrupt each other

d. not engage in side conversations

e. not repeat what has already been said

f. not "play to the audience" or monopolize the discussion

g. support the president's efforts to facilitate an orderly meeting

h. communicate openly and actively in discussion and dialog to avoid surprises

i. encourage equal participation of all members

j. practice respectful body language.

2.6. The Board will use a consent agenda as a means to expedite the disposition of routine matters and dispose of other items of business it chooses not to discuss. All administrative matters delegated to the CEO that are required by law to be approved by the Board will be acted upon by the Board via the consent agenda.

2.7. An item may be removed from the consent agenda upon approval of a majority of the Board members present and voting.

2.8. The Board, by majority vote, may revise or amend its policies at any time. However, as a customary practice, a proposed policy revision will be discussed at one session of the Board prior to being approved at a subsequent Board meeting.

Monitoring Method: Board self-assessment

Monitoring Frequency: Annually in _____

The Aspen Group International, LLC

EXHIBIT 4.2

GC-3

Policy Type: Governance Culture

Board Job Description

The Board's job is to represent, lead, and serve the owners and to govern the organization by establishing expectations for organizational results, expectations for quality operational performance, and monitoring actual performance against those expectations.

The Board will:

3.1. Ensure that the Results are the dominant focus of organizational performance.

3.2. Advocate for the organization and the clients it serves.

3.3. Initiate and maintain constructive two-way dialog with the owners and stakeholders as a means to engage all stakeholders in the work of the Board and the organization.

3.4. Develop written governing policies that address:

   a. *Results:* The intended outcomes for the clients served by the organization;

   b. *Operational Expectations:* Statements of the Board's values about operational matters delegated to the CEO, including both actions and conditions to be accomplished and those prohibited;

   c. *Governance Culture:* Definition of the Board's own work, the processes it will employ, and conditions within which it will accomplish that work;

    d. *Board-CEO Relationship*: The role relationship of the CEO and the Board, including the specified authority of the CEO and the process for monitoring organizational and CEO performance.

3.5. Ensure acceptable CEO performance through effective monitoring of Results and Operational Expectations policies.

3.6. Ensure acceptable Board performance through effective evaluation of Board actions and processes.

3.7. Appoint an independent auditor to conduct an annual external review of the organization's financial condition and report directly to the Board.

Adopted:

Monitoring Method: Board self-assessment

Monitoring Frequency: Annually in _____

The Aspen Group International, LLC

5

The Board's Relationship with Its CEO—Part 1

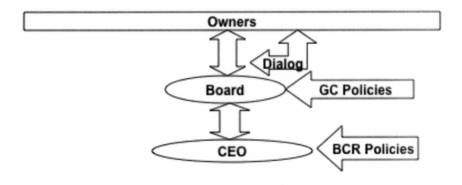

In all our years of work with boards as association trainers and advocates, a disproportionate amount of time was devoted to the challenge of helping boards and their CEOs resolve conflicts between them. More often than not, the basis for conflict centered on communication. It was common for communication problems to be the product of role confusion between the board and CEO.

The age-old, seemingly irresolvable dilemma that divides boards and CEOs has been the challenge to define roles in such a way that there is complete clarity of responsibilities.

We do know that our years of trying to help boards and CEOs reach that state of complete clarity, using traditional mind-sets, failed. We would spend a full day or more trying to help both parties reach agreement about who does what, plaster the walls with flip charts full of agreements, and leave thinking we had made some headway toward achieving role clarity. Typically we would not make it through the week before the agreements ran headlong into every-day reality, and confusion once again reigned.

We spoke in chapter 1 about the misguided understanding of the team-work concept on the part of some boards and their CEOs, who seem to believe that good teamwork means that both parties share in making the same deci-sions. We say here again that if both the board and the CEO participate in making the same decisions, one should expect role confusion; it is built into such a process.

The solution is to define roles in such a way that both the board and the CEO play complementary, but completely separate, roles.

Coherent Governance makes few promises because so much rests on the integrity of its implementation and the good faith and determination of the people who implement it. But it does make this one promise: if it is imple-mented correctly, any confusion between the roles of the board and the CEO will be eliminated once and for all.

That's a bold commitment, we understand. We will see what makes it pos-sible in chapter 8.

BOARD-CEO RELATIONSHIP POLICIES

Board-CEO Relationship (BCR) policies are the glue that holds Coherent Governance together. These (typically) five policies may be viewed as the "Coherent" part of Coherent Governance; without them, there would be no complete system concept. There would be only pieces of a system that may have some value in themselves, but they would stop well short of completing the complex puzzle of good governance.

Coherent Governance is based largely on what most people long have con-sidered to be simply good governing practice. Among those traditional good practices is the principle that, regardless of the type of organization, whether public or private, large or small, for profit or not for profit, the board controls the organization through the single throttle point of the CEO.

When boards practice this principle, things seem to work. When boards go beyond or around the CEO and start directing or managing staff at other levels, problems are imminent.

BCR policies serve the purpose of clarifying the board's role as it relates to the CEO's role. They centralize in the position of CEO complete responsibility for the success or failure of the organization, But, along with significant accountability comes significant authority, within the board's stated values.

The typical five BCR policies, which work in any organization, regardless of type or size, are as follows:

BCR-1: Single Point of Direction
The board recognizes the CEO to be the only link between the board and the operational organization.

BCR-2: Single Unit of Control
The board commits to govern as a group, allowing no individual to give personal direction or to demand work personally.

BCR-3: Staff Accountability
All staff matters belong to the CEO. The board commits to stay out of all staff issues, except as may be required by law (for certain public boards).

BCR-4: Delegation of Authority
How will the board provide direction to the CEO? What is the CEO's level of authority?

BCR-5: Monitoring CEO Performance
For what is the CEO responsible? How will the CEO be evaluated?

This chapter is divided into two sections, for a purpose: there is no way the full range of concepts embodied in the BCR section can be outlined until the next two quadrants are presented. Following chapters 6 and 7, we will return in chapter 8 to this discussion of Board-CEO Relationships, and spend more time discussing primarily the concepts represented by these last two policies, BCR-4 and BCR-5.

SUMMARY
Confusion of roles between the board and CEO usually leads to communication issues, which lead to disintegration of the relationship. It is possible to achieve complete clarity of roles, provided model rules are followed. Coherent

Governance is based on established principles of good governance and is not radical in concept.

QUESTIONS FOR THOUGHT

1. What has been your organization's experience with regard to role clarity between the board and the CEO?
2. How do you react to the idea that the CEO should be responsible for the success or failure of the organization?
3. At this point in the book, do you believe it is possible for boards and CEOs to achieve indisputable clarity of roles?

Controlling Operational Decisions without Helping the CEO Manage

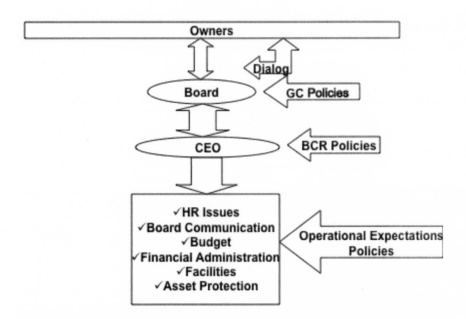

Every day, within the operational side of all organizations, hundreds of "things" happen. People are hired, trained, evaluated, disciplined, rewarded, and fired; money is budgeted, invested, and spent; buildings are constructed, renovated, used, and maintained; customers and clients are related to, sometimes appropriately, sometimes not; operational strategies intended to produce desired results are planned and implemented.

All boards have concerns about these things. And every board has an obligation, on behalf of the owners it serves, to assure that the organization operates soundly and within the board's own values. To delegate the full spectrum of operational decision making without defining the boundaries within which such decisions are made is dereliction of duty on the part of the board.

But while the board's concern about operational decision making is proper and necessary, the way the board goes about exercising reasonable and appropriate diligence is where things normally go wrong.

COMMITTEES

For example, many boards form committees focused on operational functions (finance, personnel, curriculum, facilities, etc.) as vehicles to "help" management make reasonable decisions about such functions or to "oversee" the decisions that are made. This misuse of committees is evidence of a fundamental lack of understanding of the board's role. A number of bad things can result from this kind of committee utilization:

1. The full board can be lulled into believing that the committee is so diligent that other members can trust it to do work that rightfully belongs to the full board;
2. A few members tend to become more knowledgeable than others about a functional area and can develop an unhealthy level of ownership. This uneven knowledge and understanding can result in decisions about which sometimes the majority of the members are poorly informed;
3. Individual members tend to yield their vote to the opinion or direction of the expert member;
4. This ownership can impact staff in negative ways, creating the impression by staff that they are obligated to take direction from and to please not their CEO, but rather the committee or its chair;
5. Worse, fiefdoms can be created where individual members are the "knowledge experts," sometimes even superseding the knowledge and work of professional staff.

There are legitimate places for board committees, but using them to oversee the work of staff in operational areas, or to help staff do the work that they normally know how to do better than the board or its committees, is not among them.

Board committees should be used to help the board do board work, not to help the staff do staff work. If operationally focused committees are needed, their creation should be based on the CEO's initiative, and they should be staff committees reporting to the CEO, not the board.

RECOMMENDATION-APPROVAL GAME

We have spoken already about the problems associated with the traditional CEO recommendation-board approval exchange, in which virtually every significant operational decision is submitted by the CEO to the board for the board to approve. Public entities, especially public school boards, seem to have accepted the belief that this is the only way important decisions can be made. The role of the CEO and staff is simply to construct the best recommendation they can, and rely on the wisdom of the board to say whether the proposed decision is worthy or not.

In fact, graduate schools for years taught that this type of CEO-board relationship was good and proper, and was the way important decisions were expected to be made. According to this theory, the basis for judging whether a decision belonged to the CEO or the board was the level of importance assigned to the decision, without regard to the nature of the decision itself. In other words, if a decision rises to a certain level of importance, it belongs to the board, not to the CEO; the CEO can make only relatively unimportant decisions.

For highly educated and trained executives, who in most cases have been hired by the board because of their impressive credentials and their apparent leadership qualities, to be told that they cannot do the jobs for which they were hired until the board says so is demeaning.

Even if this were a defensible way to make operational decisions, it remains fraught with problems. Once a decision is made by board approval, that is the direction the organization is headed, regardless of changing circumstance. If conditions within the organization change, as they invariably will at some point, additional board action is required before the organization can respond to these changes. The organization is hamstrung by such limiting conditions.

We spoke earlier about the issue of confused accountability, but it is so important we will say it again: if both the board and the CEO share in making the same decision via this recommendation-approval game, neither or both are accountable for the result of the decision.

The simple rule is: the party who makes the decision should be held accountable for the results of the decision.

Shared decision making may sound good and have some level of appeal in some contexts, but in terms of the board-CEO relationship, shared decision making causes nothing but confusion. Good conversation about important decisions is commendable and perfectly appropriate, but at the end of the dialog, someone must make a decision and accept the accompanying responsibility for its results.

CLARIFYING THE BOARD'S VALUES IN ADVANCE

Let's recap: it is appropriate for the board to have concerns about all kinds of operational matters. But it is inappropriate for the board to exercise control of the organization or provide oversight by using committees or by approving all important decisions about operational matters. If the board should not do its work by committees overseeing staff work or by reserving final decisions for itself, then just how does a board control operational decision making and assure that decisions conform to the board's values?

Try this: let's assume that you are a member of a school board, and your superintendent is bringing to you for your approval a recommendation about a new school district calendar for the next school year. It is likely that if certain conditions did not exist, you would find yourself unable to support the recommendation. What are those factors that would cause you to oppose the recommendation and vote against the calendar?

Let's assume that your personal values about the school district calendar are these: the overall best interests of students must be served; the school year should start no earlier than Labor Day; the first semester should end before the Christmas-New Year's break; the school year should end no later than June 1; and the proposed calendar should have been reviewed by staff and parents representing a good cross-section of the two groups. If any of these conditions were not reflected in the recommendation, you would be inclined to oppose the CEO's recommendation to approve the calendar.

Now let's assume that all of your personal concerns about the calendar are shared by the majority of your board colleagues. In such case, why not write down this set of board values about the school district calendar, creating a board policy about this topic? If your CEO and staff know in advance what criteria the board expects to use to assess the recommendation, they no longer must guess what would satisfy the board. The "target" is defined.

But let's take this example one step farther. If the board has clarified its expectations in advance in written policy, why would it need to approve the school calendar at all? If all the conditions specified in the board's policy had been met, what more should the board expect? Why wouldn't the CEO present to the board a report providing hard evidence that when the calendar was developed, the board's criteria were understood and complied with? The board may use the report as a vehicle to judge whether the CEO and staff had complied with the board's values about the school district calendar, without having to approve the calendar at all.

Repeatedly over the years we have seen school boards consume weeks and months wrangling over this very matter, rehashing the very same issues year after year. They never think of taking the time to resolve sometimes-conflicting board member values about the calendar at one time, then commit the group's shared values to policy, which could drive decision making about that issue every time it is faced.

And the by-product of this method is that it allows the board to control the content and process of developing the school calendar without being required to consider and approve the calendar itself.

This example is one that allows us to make the point that the board is not required to make decisions—or even share in their making—in order to control them. By anticipating in advance the factors that would cause the board to reject administrative recommendations and then committing them to policy, the board sets the parameters within which operational decisions are made. It is controlling without deciding.

HOW MUCH CAN AND SHOULD THE BOARD CONTROL?

If boards choose to govern the organization this way, how should they decide how much to control directly versus how much to delegate? The board, after all, is the board. Within legal constraints, the board could assume complete control of the organization, if it chose to do so.

But boards were never intended to be in charge of anything other than themselves. *The board's role is to govern the organization, not to manage it—or even to manage the manager.*

There is a fundamental difference between the role of governance and the role of administration. The difference is not a matter of degree, but a matter of function.

The *governance function* is one of translating the needs and expectations of the ownership into policy directives that guide decision making throughout the operational organization. The role of *administration* is to assure that the organization operates in a manner consistent with the board's policies and that it produces the results for owners and clients specified by the board in policy.

Board members are not expected to understand the intricacies of organizational management. It is not necessary to have that much ground-level understanding in order to be effective board members. What is important is for the board to have governing systems in place to enable it to delegate with confidence that its values are being observed as operational decisions are made.

Common sense suggests that if the board can do the job of running the organization as well as its CEO, it may have the wrong CEO.

Nevertheless, there are certain operational decisions that the board may choose to reserve for itself, for whatever good reason. The discussion about which to delegate and which to reserve for the board always is an interesting one. We come down on the side of advising the board to delegate as much as it is willing to delegate—and concomitantly assign as much accountability as it can.

Our conviction is that the more the board delegates, the more powerful the board becomes—as long as the board has done an adequate job of establishing the parameters within which delegated decision making will occur and building monitoring systems to effectively assess organizational performance.

COHERENT GOVERNANCE VS. OTHER MODELS

Some governance models tend to be so rigid that they try to confine the board to a very narrow set of operational expectations. If the board has concerns about an operational issue outside the bounds of "the formula," the board is told that it is improper for it to have any say in such matters.

We reject that argument outright. To tell a school board that it cannot say anything about the instructional program, or student discipline, or the learning environment, is beyond our comprehension. All boards have such concerns, and those concerns will be expressed, if not in advance in policy, then later as the second-guessing begins about operations the board has said nothing about.

This is one of the most fundamental differences between Coherent Governance and other similar models. We come down on the side of encouraging the board to "stake out its turf" in policy about any operational issue with which it has concern, to whatever level of concern it has, and then get out of operational decision making about those issues and delegate the rest to the CEO.

This is a defensible way to allow the board to exercise reasonable control over operational decisions. Relegating the board to a bystander role in such areas of organizational decision making is not something we can defend.

Coherent Governance allows the board to reserve as much decision-making authority for itself as it must, about any operational matter, in order to confidently delegate the rest to its CEO. There are no limitations to this concept. The caveat is that if the board makes the decisions, it, not the CEO, is accountable for the results.

We'll say again that the more the board delegates, the more powerful it becomes. And in reverse, the more decisions the board retains for itself, the less accountability it assigns to its CEO—and the more the board's decisions can limit the CEO's range of choices to make expected results happen.

We encourage boards to think in terms of how much authority they can delegate, not how much they can retain.

We use the simple graphic of a continuum to illustrate the concept of delegation of authority. The box on the next page shows how the choice of delegation is defined: Wherever the board stakes out its degree of reserved authority, from that point forward it delegates any additional related decision making and authority to its CEO.

The board always controls as much as it must in order to confidently delegate authority to its CEO. Again, the board could completely fill up the continuum with reserved board authority, leaving little or no room for the CEO to exercise authority.

For example, the board conceivably could say that the CEO may make no decision about the school district calendar without the board's approval. (The line would be filled with xxx's with no room remaining for professional judgment.) Few boards choose this degree of direct authority, however, so somewhere short of that extreme is where the board will land.

The Continuum of Decision Making
The board, through its policies, establishes its operational standards. Once the board has articulated all its values and written them down in an Operational Expectations policy (the area in the diagram represented by "x"), the CEO then assumes authority to make all further related decisions, as long as they do not conflict with the board's values.

Logically, once the CEO has finished defining his or her standards, those who report at a lower level will be able to make even more related decisions, as long as they don't conflict with anything said by the board or CEO in their respective areas of decision making. This is systems thinking at work!

Example: School safety
Board: CEO will permit no unsafe conditions anywhere within the organization.
CEO: Every school site will have an approved safety plan.
Site Administrative Staff: All schools will have monitored video cameras throughout the building, all outside entrances will be locked except for the main entrance, and armed guards will be on duty while the building is occupied.

Board   CEO   Administrative Staff
_____

xxxxxxxxxxxxxxx / 0000000000000 / ********************

This concept provides the single best means we know to establish absolute role clarity between the board and the CEO. The board always has control over the decision about what and how much to delegate, but if the board has not reserved a specific decision for itself, then by definition that decision belongs to the CEO. There should be no confusion about who gets to make which decision.

THE TEENAGER ANALOGY
Sometimes new concepts become easier to grasp if we analogize them to familiar examples. Let's assume that you are leaving your sixteen-year-old son

home alone for the first time while you and your spouse attend a weekend function fifty miles away. He is a mature young man, and you are confident that he can handle himself as you expect.

Still, there are certain instructions you wish to convey, just to be sure that he understands your expectations of him. What kinds of expectations will you express? Let's try these:

1. While we are away, we expect you to have no parties here at the house.
2. We expect that you will have no female visitors.
3. The liquor cabinet is off limits.
4. If you go out with friends, we expect you to be home at the same time you would be home if we were here.
5. The trash should be taken out for pickup.
6. Be sure to feed the dog.
7. In general, we expect you to comply with the same family values you know and understand, as if we were here.

Do these instructions sound reasonable? Are they comprehensive enough that you now feel secure that your expectations will be understood and complied with?

When you return, you may monitor his behavior to be sure that it conformed to your expectations (more about this in chapter 9), but you probably can leave with some measure of comfort that your sixteen-year-old is capable of managing himself while you are away.

This is the very same process a board would use to convey instructions to its CEO about operational conditions and circumstances within the organization. The board likely would not tolerate certain actions and conditions, if they occurred. These conditions and actions should be prohibited by specific policy language.

For example, the board might find it unacceptable for the CEO to permit any unsafe conditions to exist in the workplace (think British Petroleum); or the board likely would find it unacceptable for assets of the organization to go unprotected (think intellectual properties). These conditions, then, would be prohibited by policy.

If certain conditions and actions did not exist, the board likely would find their absence to be unacceptable. For example, the board probably would not be willing to accept the absence of an effective employee evaluation system, or the CEO's failure to assure that all employees are trained and prepared to do the jobs for which they were hired. These conditions, then, are required of the CEO.

Most Operational Expectations policies have two sections. The first provides direction to the CEO about those conditions and actions the board requires to exist or have in place; the second prohibits the actions and conditions the board would find unacceptable. Thus for every operational area, the board states in policy either "do this" or "don't do this."

If the board wishes to reserve for itself any particular decision, it prohibits the CEO from making that decision. For example, the board may say that the CEO may not sell fixed assets of the organization. The result of establishing this prohibition is that only the board can make the decision about disposal of fixed assets.

Once the board has provided all the guidance it feels necessary about the specific topic, the board at that point delegates any additional decision making about that topic to the CEO.

It is this process that establishes complete clarity of roles between the board and the CEO. The board always controls the decision about how much authority to delegate, but once the board has staked out its turf in policy, the CEO's authority begins.

The first objective of this kind of governing role for the board is to establish absolute clarity of roles and separation of responsibility between the board and the CEO. Good teamwork does not require the two to make the same decision, or even to collaborate in making a decision. Good teamwork does require them to play complementary roles and to honor the role played by the other.

The second objective is clear accountability for the decisions that are made. For CEOs, this freedom to make important decisions without the board's blessing is exceptionally rewarding and freeing, but the corresponding accountability for the results of those decisions can be an uncomfortable fit for the CEO who lacks competence or confidence.

The "safety net" of board approval has been removed. No longer can the CEO point to the board as the party that had its hands on the decision last, and therefore shares at least a part of the blame for a bad decision.

OPERATIONAL EXPECTATIONS POLICY TOPICS

The number of issues to be covered in OE policies, to some extent, depends upon the type of organization the board governs.

For example, every organization of whatever type will need a policy dealing with financial planning and with financial administration. If you are a school board, you likely will choose to develop policies dealing with the instructional program, student discipline, and others specific to education. If you are an insurance pool board, you probably will elect to have operational policies dealing with loss control, risk management, and a few others specific to your industry. If you are a health care organization, you might recognize the need for policies dealing with admissions, payment expectations, and provider qualifications.

The base set of Operational Expectations policies includes the following:

OE-1: Global Operational Expectation

This policy is the broadest, most universal statement of operational expectations the board can make, and it is stated prohibitively. The board will not permit any operational condition that is unlawful, unethical, imprudent, disrespectful, unsafe, and so on. All other OE policies flow from this one and are statements further defining the values stated in OE-1.

OE-2: Emergency CEO Succession

This policy becomes important only when it is needed, and that cannot be predicted. It requires a succession plan in the event of an unforeseen emergency.

OE-3: Treatment of Owners and Stakeholders

The board has values about how it expects people to be treated. What are those values? How much definition does the board need to provide in order to be assured that everyone within the organization understands these values?

OE-4: Personnel Administration

What kinds of employees does the board expect to serve the organization? What values does the board hold about employee qualifications, evaluation, staff development, compensation, and other related issues?

OE-5: Budget and Financial Planning

The budget is considered to be a management tool, but the board has some reasonable concerns about it. How much risk will be tolerated in revenue forecasting? How should the budget be related to the board's goals and priorities for the year? How should the budget be presented to the board, if the board is required by law to approve it? Does the board value a planned year-end fund balance? If so, how much?

OE-6: Financial Administration

After the budget is adopted, how are the dollars to be handled? What are the board's values about paying bills and payroll obligations on time? About financial record keeping? About investment practice? Are employees who handle money expected to be bonded?

OE-7: Asset Protection

Virtually all organizations own assets of various types, ranging from a computer and printer to millions of dollars invested in large equipment, buildings, land, and other hard assets. How does the board expect these assets to be cared for and protected?

OE-8: Communicating with the Board

When relationships between the board and the CEO deteriorate, communication issues usually can be found somewhere near the root of the problem. What are the board's expectations of the CEO in terms of the frequency and types of communication that should be provided?

OE-9: Communicating with the Owners

The board itself has a large role to play in communicating with the organization's owners, but so do the CEO and staff, especially in public organizations such as school districts, cities, counties, and others. What are the board's expectations about how the CEO is to carry out this external communication function?

We have included two sample OE policies as exhibits 6.1 and 6.2. As stated above, other policies will be necessary for certain organizations, depending upon the nature of the organization itself. But the foregoing policy topics are fairly universal, in our experience, and serve as the baseline for additional work by the board to flesh out policies expressing its values about organizational behavior.

Remember, once the board completes the task of creating OE policies, it then hands off to the CEO the responsibility to do the job he or she was hired to do, but within these stated OE policy values. Any other decision that needs to be made within any of these topic areas is the CEO's to make. Thus it is important that the board carefully and prudently control operations to its comfort level before delegating additional decision making to the CEO.

SUMMARY

All boards have concerns about how effectively and efficiently the organizations they govern operate. In the exercise of their oversight of these organizations, many boards use committees to "help" the CEO do their assigned work, and also insist on approving virtually every important CEO decision as a means to control the organization's decision making. The result of using committees in this way is fragmentation of the board and confusion by staff about whom they serve. The result of the board's approving operational decisions made by the CEO is confused roles and accountability.

A better way to control operational decisions without making them via the approval process is to define the board's values about operational decisions in advance, commit them to policy, and then delegate decisions to the CEO within the board's stated values. The board can control the organization to the board's level of concern, through policy, without sharing in decision making through the approval process.

QUESTIONS FOR THOUGHT

1. Does your board use committees to oversee staff work?
2. Does your board approve most important operational decisions, even though the CEO is considered to be responsible for the functions in question?
3. Is it clear to you who is accountable for decisions that have been approved by the board based upon a CEO recommendation?

EXHIBIT 6.1

OE-5

Policy Type: Operational Expectations
Financial Planning
The CEO shall develop and maintain a multi-year financial plan that is related directly to the Board's Results priorities and Operational Expectations goals, and that avoids long-term fiscal jeopardy to the organization.

The CEO will develop a budget that:
5.1. Is in a summary format understandable to the Board and presented in a manner that allows the Board to understand the relationship between the budget and the Results priorities and any Operational Expectations goals for the year.
5.2. Credibly describes revenues and expenditures.
5.3. Shows the amount spent in each budget category for the most recently completed fiscal year, the amount budgeted for the current fiscal year, and the amount budgeted for the next fiscal year.
5.4. Discloses budget-planning assumptions.
5.5. Assures fiscal soundness in future years.
5.6. Reflects anticipated changes in employee compensation, including inflationary adjustments, step increases, performance increases, and benefits.
5.7. Includes amounts determined by the Board to be necessary for the Board to effectively and efficiently perform its governing responsibilities.
The CEO may not develop a budget that:
5.8. Plans for the expenditure in any fiscal year of more funds than are conservatively projected to be available during the year.
5.9. Provides for an anticipated year-end fund balance of less than

_____.

Adopted:
Monitoring Method: Internal Report
Monitoring Frequency: Annually in _____
The Aspen Group International, LLC

EXHIBIT 6.2

OE-12

Policy Type: Operational Expectations

Facilities

The CEO shall assure that physical facilities support the accomplishment of the Board's Results policies.

The CEO will:

12.1. Maintain a plan that establishes priorities for construction, renovation, and maintenance projects and that:

  a. Assigns highest priority to the correction of unsafe conditions;

  b. Includes maintenance costs as necessary to enable facilities to reach their intended life cycles;

  c. Plans for and schedules preventive maintenance;

  d. Plans for and schedules system replacement when new facilities open, buildings are renovated, or systems are replaced;

  e. Discloses assumptions on which the plan is based, including growth patterns and the financial and human impact individual projects will have on other parts of the organization.

12.2. Project life-cycle costs as capital decisions are made.

12.3. Assure that facilities are safe, clean, and properly maintained.

12.4. Develop and consistently administer facilities use guidelines delineating:

  a. Permitted uses;

  b. The applicable fee structure;

  c. Clear user expectations, including behavior, cleanup, security, insurance, and damage repair;

  d. Consequences and enforcement procedures for outside users who fail to follow the established rules.

The CEO may not:

12.5. Build or renovate buildings.

12.6. Recommend land acquisition without first determining growth patterns, comparative costs, construction and transportation factors, and any extraordinary contingency costs due to potential natural and man-made risks.

12.7. Authorize construction schedules and change orders that significantly increase cost or reduce quality.

12.8. Unreasonably deny the use of facilities by other parties as long as the primary needs of the organization and its clients are not compromised.

Adopted:

Monitoring Method: Internal report

Monitoring Frequency: Annually in _____

The Aspen Group International, LLC

Becoming a Results-
Driven Organization

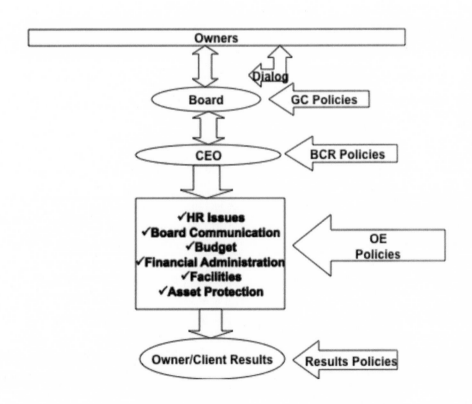

Who are your clients? Are they the same people as your owners, or are they different?

If you serve on the board of directors of a membership organization—a trade union, for example—it is likely that you would conclude that the owners and clients are the same: your members. If you serve as a member of a city council, you might define the ownership as the residents or citizens of the city, and decide that the clients are the same people. It isn't quite that simple, but we'll come back to the complications in a moment.

If you serve on a public school board, you likely would agree that your owners are the residents or citizens of the school district, but your clients are their children who enroll in your schools. If your owners and clients are different, how does your board balance the sometimes-conflicting expectations of the owners with the needs of the clients? Which side of this tension-filled debate do you believe the board should come down on?

But even in our city council example, are the owners and clients really the same people? When does an owner become a client? Are all owners full-time clients, or do owners change hats when they need and expect a specific service or benefit for themselves that other elements of the ownership may not need or want at that time? How does a board recognize when it is talking to an owner, and when it is talking with a client?

This isn't intended to be a dizzying array of questions designed to complicate readers' lives, but answering these questions is a step that the board must take. One way or the other, the questions will be answered, either deliberately and thoughtfully, or on the fly, as issues inevitably confront the board. Reasoned answers to these basic questions are necessary before the board can progress to the real challenge discussed in this chapter: defining the results the organization is expected to achieve for the clients, on behalf of the owners.

But the board must be clear about to whom it is accountable (the owners), and it must have no doubt about the identity of its clients, before this heavy work can begin. We cannot answer the questions posed above in any blanket fashion, and certainly not in a book meant for a broad readership. These are issues each board must address individually.

Here are a couple of basic questions to ponder: Why does your organization exist? Would the world be any better or worse if it didn't?

If we base an answer to these questions on what we usually see when we observe a board meeting, we likely would conclude that the organization exists so that employees will be happy; or so that we can operate efficiently and effectively; or so that buildings will be modern and well equipped; or so that the budget will be balanced; or so the color of the buildings will be acceptable to most members of the board. These are the things we see many boards spending their time debating and deciding.

Let's all agree that happy employees, efficient and effective operations, modern and well-equipped buildings, balanced budgets, and aesthetically pleasing facilities all are important and desirable.

But are these the real reasons why an organization exists? Aren't all these desirable conditions aimed at something bigger and more important? Don't the owners expect something meaningful to happen for themselves or for the clients the organization serves as a result of these desirable conditions? What are those expected outcomes?

Defining the expected outcomes the organization commits to provide, and then monitoring performance to judge whether it is happening, are components of the most important work a board can do. But it usually isn't the work most boards do.

Boards typically consume themselves with attention to operational issues that should be delegated to the CEO (see chapter 6), and in the course of doing so ignore altogether the reason the organization exists: to make life better for the owners and clients. Anything related to results they tend to leave to staff, and in so doing they give away the best part of their jobs.

RESULTS: THE DOMINANT FOCUS

The fourth and final piece to the Coherent Governance model is Results policies. As we have discussed, most boards tend to devote precious little time and attention to organizational results, but they really should be the centerpiece of everything the organization—and the board—does. A high-performing board will spend half its meeting time, at least, discussing results: Where is the organization succeeding? Where is it not? Why not? What needs to change in order to improve performance?

These can be exciting conversations, much more so than bricks, budgets, boundaries, boilers, bonds, and buses. If the board has set the boundaries of operational performance through careful crafting of the Operational Expectations policies, and if the organization can demonstrate performance consistent with those policy values, there is no reason why the board cannot shift its major attention to the results and whether the organization is making reasonable progress toward their achievement.

CRAFTING RESULTS POLICIES

Unlike policies in the other three quadrants, Results policies are built from the ground up. They are blank-page, blue-sky work, rather than using templates as a starting point. We suggest that members of the board consciously assume the "owners' proxy" role when deciding what Results policies should be. They should try to see the world through the eyes of an owner and answer the question, "What am I buying from the organization that is worth the cost?"

In order to help boards grab hold of the task, we suggest that the board begin its consideration of possible Results with the phrase, "As a result of our efforts, (clients) will . . . " Of course, the "our" refers to the entire organization, from the board throughout the operational side of the organization. We use this lead-in phrase to help the board avoid falling off onto the strategy or operational side of the fence, and instead focus on outcomes.

Let's use a school board example as we explore possible Results policies. And let's agree that the community and its citizens are our owners and students are our clients—the reason why the district exists. The exercise we recommended above would go something like this: "As a result of our efforts, students will . . . " The board should decide what students will do, or be able to do, as a result of their school experience.

The blank may be completed with such possible outcomes as:

- Read at grade level
- Be contributing citizens
- Be prepared to succeed in the workplace
- Be technologically literate

These all are legitimate outcomes and could constitute reasonable results that owners expect the school district to produce for their clients, the students.

Some boards succumb to the temptation to use such weak phrases as "be exposed to," or "participate in," or "have the opportunity to" when considering results possibilities.

Avoid all of these, and any other such activity-based language. Why? They are not outcomes; they are things the organization will do, not what the student (in this example) will be able to do.

If responses begin to flow toward any of these activities, ask "why." Why would you want students to "participate in"? Or "be exposed to"? Or "have the opportunity to"? The answer to the "why" question will get you to the true outcome level that you seek.

Let us acknowledge here that this is one of the most challenging parts of policy development since it is blank-page work and since many boards are so unaccustomed to living in the world of results.

Perhaps the main reason why many boards spend so much time focused on operations and not on results is that operations are relatively simple compared with results. Everybody knows—or thinks he knows—something about virtually every operational issue and usually is comfortable discussing such matters. Results are a different challenge, especially for boards such as school boards that are populated by laymen, elected to office, and who now find themselves involved in discussions that fall outside their comfort zone.

Nevertheless, skills can be developed, and the more board members live in the world of results, the more comfortable they become doing so. This can be the most rewarding work a board can do, once they are engaged in it.

We have included at the end of this chapter some actual Results policies from three boards: the Fairfax County, Virginia, School Board (exhibit 7.1); Enduris, a self-insurance pool in Spokane, Washington (exhibit 7.2); and Nikkei Concerns, an elder-care organization in Seattle (exhibit 7.3).

SUMMARY

Boards must be absolutely clear about the identities of their owners and their clients. Owners and clients may be the same people, or they can be different. Results policies should drive all organizational focus and decisions on behalf of the clients you exist to serve. They are built from the ground up, using no templates. Results policies are outcomes for clients and are the world in which the board should live.

QUESTIONS FOR THOUGHT

1. Is your board clear about the identity of its ownership and its clients?
2. Do board-defined results drive what your organization does? If not, what does?
3. How much time does your board spend on results? On operations?

EXHIBIT 7.1: FAIRFAX, VIRGINIA, SCHOOL BOARD RESULTS POLICIES

Student Achievement Goals

1. Academics

   All students will obtain, understand, analyze, communicate, and apply knowledge and skills to achieve success in school and in life. Students will:

   1.1. Achieve their full academic potential in the core disciplines of:

      1.1.1. English language arts:
      - Reading.
      - Writing.
      - Communication.

      1.1.2. Math.

      1.1.3. Science.

      1.1.4 Social studies.

   1.2. Communicate in at least two languages.

   1.3. Explore, understand, and value the fine and practical arts.

   1.4. Understand the interrelationship and interdependence of the countries and cultures of the world.

   1.5. Effectively use technology to access, communicate, and apply knowledge and to foster creativity.

2. Essential Life Skills

   All students will demonstrate the aptitude, attitude, and skills to lead responsible, fulfilling, and respectful lives. Working in partnership with school and family, students will:

   2.1. Demonstrate sound moral character and ethical judgment:

      2.1.1. Model honesty and integrity.

      2.1.2. Take responsibility for their actions.

      2.1.3. Keep their promises and commitments.

      2.1.4. Respect people, property, and authority.

      2.1.5. Exercise good stewardship of the environment.

      2.1.6. Protect others' health and safety.

      2.1.7. Show respect and understanding for the interests and opinions of others.

      2.1.8. Be capable of placing their own self-interests in perspective with the interests of others.

   2.2. Be able to contribute effectively within a group dynamic.

2.3. Develop the resilience and self-confidence required to deal effectively with life's challenges.

2.4. Possess the skills to manage and resolve conflict.

2.5. Be inspired to learn throughout life.

2.6. Courageously identify and pursue their personal goals.

2.7. Develop practical life skills including but not limited to:

    2.7.1. Problem solving/critical thinking.

    2.7.2. Work habits and ethics.

    2.7.3. Financial competency.

    2.7.4. Self-sufficiency.

    2.7.5. Time management.

2.8. Make healthy and safe life choices.

3. Responsibility to the Community

All students will understand and model the important attributes that people must have to contribute to an effective and productive community and the common good of all. Students will:

3.1. Know and practice the duties, responsibilities, and rights of citizenship in a democratic society.

3.2. Be respectful and contributing participants in their school, community, country, and world.

3.3. Understand the purpose, role, and means of interaction with the different levels of government.

Adopted:

Monitoring Method: Internal Report

Monitoring Frequency: As determined annually by the Board

EXHIBIT 7.2: ENDURIS BOARD OF DIRECTORS, SPOKANE, WASHINGTON, RESULTS POLICIES

Policy Type: Results

R-1 Mega Result

Members have long-term financial protection from property and liability loss. Members will:

R:2 Enjoy competitive, stable, and understandable rates.

R:3 Enjoy competent, responsive, fair, and balanced claims administration, including peer review when appropriate.

R:4 Realize cost advantages resulting from effective management of their own risks.

R:5 Enjoy comprehensive coverage influenced by their needs.

R:6 Share in the financial stability of Enduris and have confidence in its governance, management, and long-term viability.

Adopted:

Monitoring Method: Internal Report

Monitoring Frequency: As determined annually by the Board

EXHIBIT 7.3: NIKKEI CONCERNS BOARD OF DIRECTORS, SEATTLE, WASHINGTON, RESULTS POLICIES

Policy Type: Results

Mission

Our mission is to enrich and support the lives of elders and meet their needs in a way that honors and respects Nikkei culture and values.

R.1 The lives of our elders are enriched and supported in a way that honors and respects Nikkei culture and values.

R.2 Our elderly will maintain the highest possible quality of life, including physical and mental health and wellness.

R.3 Our elderly will sustain their independence as much as possible.

R.4 Our elderly will lead socially and culturally enriched lives in a warm and welcoming environment.

R.5 Our elderly will have peace of mind, feeling safe and nurtured.

Owners = Nikkei Community of Greater Seattle

Clients = Nikkei elders

Adopted:

Monitoring Method: Internal Report

Monitoring Frequency: As determined annually by the Board

| 8 |

The Board's Relationship with Its CEO—Part 2

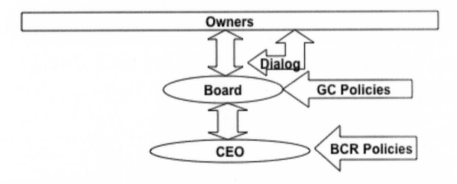

Let's do a quick review of the last three chapters. In chapter 5, we started a discussion of the board's relationship with the CEO and the policies usually found in the Board-CEO Relationship (BCR) section of Coherent Governance policies. We temporarily set aside some of the specifics about that topic, promising to return to that discussion after chapters 6 and 7.

In chapter 6, we discussed Operational Expectations policies, a means by which the board can control all operational decisions, in policy, without the necessity of approving CEO recommendations.

In chapter 7, the focus was on Results policies, which are intended to describe the board's outcome expectations for the clients served by the organization.

Now with these additional two concepts described, we're ready to return to the Board-CEO Relationship policies for a final look.

Why was it necessary to interrupt that discussion in chapter 5? This is why: The BCR policies declare that the performance of the organization and the performance of the CEO are identical. The organization is expected to do two things: all operations must comply with the board's values expressed in the Operational Expectations policies, and the organization is expected to make reasonable progress toward achieving the outcomes described in the board's Results policies.

Since the organization's performance and the CEO's performance are identical, these two components constitute the CEO's evaluation. We had to set aside the details of this concept until the OE and Results chapters were presented.

With the picture now complete, it is clear that the CEO has significant accountability well beyond the norm. But the concept is elegant in its simplicity. The CEO's job description has only two components: make reasonable progress over time toward achieving the Results, and be sure the organization operates according to the board's OE values. That's all. And those two components constitute the totality of the CEO's evaluation.

What more should a board expect of its CEO than that? If the board is clear in stating its expectations about both results and operations, why should the evaluation be based on anything else? The process of monitoring, quite obviously, takes on a prominent level of importance, since it serves the dual purpose of assessing both organizational and CEO performance.

The board will be monitoring organizational performance in these two areas each time it meets (we discuss monitoring in chapter 9), and when it does, it is building a portfolio of organizational performance; it isn't evaluating the CEO just yet. But at the end of the full year's monitoring cycle, the board takes that portfolio of organizational evaluations and credits the CEO with the results of the process.

Some people tend to reject certain features of governing models, claiming that they give too much authority to the CEO. While it is true that Coherent Governance does promote the assignment of reasonable authority to the CEO, it also is true that the CEO assumes enormous accountability for achieving operational excellence and results for clients.

Every operational decision made by the CEO and staff is aimed at producing those results. Each time a strategic choice is made, the CEO is betting on its success, realizing that his or her success rides on the outcome of the choices being made.

In our minds, that is a degree of accountability that at least balances any additional authority that may be extended to a CEO. As we have stated, a confident, secure CEO will welcome the freedom the model offers in terms of ability to do the job with minimal interference. A less secure, less confident CEO will be more comfortable having the board approve every decision—and share in the accountability for the results.

We have included as exhibit 8.1 a sample BCR policy that defines both the authority delegated to the CEO and the CEO job description.

Exhibit 8.2 is a sample policy that describes the accountability the CEO has for both operations and for results, including the CEO's evaluation criteria and process. Appendix D is an actual summative evaluation of a public school superintendent, with identification disguised for obvious reasons.

SUMMARY

The CEO has two components in his job description: achieve the results the board called for in its Results policies, and be sure the organization complies with the board's Operational Expectations values. The performance of the CEO and the performance of the organization are the same. As the board monitors organizational performance, it indirectly is monitoring and evaluating CEO performance. While Coherent Governance does encourage additional delegation of authority to the CEO, it also assigns significant accountability to the CEO for the decisions that are made.

QUESTIONS FOR THOUGHT

1. What is your reaction to the idea that the organization's performance and the CEO's performance are identical?
2. Are you comfortable with the idea that the CEO will be evaluated only on Results progress and OE compliance?
3. Is the tradeoff, added authority for added accountability, reasonable?

EXHIBIT 8.1

B/CR-4

Sample Policy Type: Board-CEO Relationship

Authority of the CEO

The Board will provide direction to the CEO through written policies that define the organizational results to be achieved for clients and define operational conditions and actions to be accomplished or avoided.

4.1. The Board will develop Results policies instructing the CEO to achieve defined results for the clients served by the organization.

4.2. The Board will develop Operational Expectations policies that express the Board's values about operational conditions and actions. Certain of these values will be expressed positively to assure that the stated actions occur and the identified conditions exist, and will be stated as directives. Certain other values represent actions and conditions that are to be avoided, and will be stated prohibitively.

4.3. As long as the CEO uses any reasonable interpretation of the Board's Results and Operational Expectations policies, the CEO is authorized to establish any additional operational policies or regulations, make any decisions, establish any practices, and develop any activities the CEO deems appropriate to achieve the Board's Results policies. The CEO is not expected to seek Board approval or authority for any such decision falling within the CEO's area of delegated authority.

4.4. The Board may change its Results and Operational Expectations policies, and in so doing shift the boundary between Board and CEO areas of responsibility. The Board will respect and support any reasonable interpretation of its policies by the CEO, even though CEO decisions may not be the decisions the Board or its members may have made.

Adopted:

Monitoring Method: Board self-assessment

Monitoring Frequency: Annually in _____

The Aspen Group International, LLC

EXHIBIT 8.2

B/CR-5

Sample Policy Type: Board-CEO Relationship

CEO Accountability

The Board considers CEO performance to be identical to organizational performance. Organizational accomplishment of the Board's Results policies, and operation according to the values expressed in the Board's Operational Expectations policies, will be considered successful CEO performance. These two components define the CEO's job responsibilities and are the basis for the CEO's performance evaluation.

5.1. The Board will determine organizational performance based upon a systematic monitoring process.

5.2. The Board will acquire monitoring data on Results and Operational Expectations policies by one or more of three methods:

    a. By Internal Report, in which the CEO submits information that certifies and documents to the Board compliance or reasonable progress;

    b. By External Review, in which an external third party selected by the Board assesses compliance or reasonable progress with applicable Board policies;

    c. By Board Inspection, in which the whole Board or a committee duly charged by the Board formally assesses compliance or reasonable progress based upon specific policy criteria.

5.3. The consistent performance standard for Operational Expectations policies shall be whether the CEO has:

    a. reasonably interpreted the policy and its subparts;

    b. complied with the provisions of the Board policy.

5.4. The consistent performance standard for Results policies shall be whether the CEO has:

    a. reasonably interpreted the policy and its subparts;

    b. made reasonable progress toward achieving the outcomes defined by the Board's Results policies.

5.5. The Board will make the final determination as to whether CEO interpretation is reasonable, whether the CEO is in compliance, and whether reasonable progress has been made. In doing so, the Board will apply the "reasonable person" standard.

5.6. All policies that instruct the CEO will be monitored according to a schedule and by a method determined by the Board and included in the Board's annual work plan. The Board may monitor any policy out of this defined sequence, if it is determined by a majority of the Board that conditions warrant monitoring at times other than those specified by the annual schedule.

5.7. Each _____, the Board will conduct a formal summative evaluation of the CEO. The summative evaluation will be based upon data collected during the year from the monitoring of Results and Operational Expectations policies. The Board will prepare a written evaluation document, which will consist of:

   a. A summary of the data derived during the year from monitoring the Board's Results and Operational Expectations policies;

   b. Conclusions based upon the Board's prior action during the year relative to the CEO's reasonable interpretation of each Result policy and whether reasonable progress has been made toward its achievement;

   c. Conclusions based upon the Board's prior action during the year relative to whether the CEO has reasonably interpreted and operated according to the provisions of the Operational Expectations policies.

Adopted:

Monitoring Method: Board self-assessment

Monitoring Frequency: Annually in _____

The Aspen Group International, LLC

9

Monitoring—Everything!

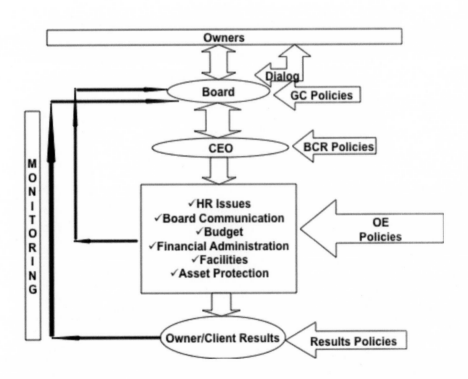

Let's recap the topics we have discussed in the last five chapters. We talked about how the board can, in policy:

- Create a governing culture for itself;
- Establish clear boundaries for executive decision making by defining the CEO's level of authority and accountability;
- Develop unambiguous expectations for all operational areas, thereby providing clear direction to the CEO and staff about every functional area; and
- Define clear outcomes the organization is expected to produce for its owners and clients.

In essence, these four quadrants of policy establish performance standards for everything and everybody associated with the organization.

- The *Governance Culture* policies set the standards of performance expected of the board itself.
- The *Board-CEO Relationship* policies establish the standards for the board in its relationship with the CEO.
- The *Operational Expectations* policies are the standards for the entire operational side of the organization.
- The *Results* policies are the outcome standards for the organization in terms of benefits for the owners and clients.

But the concept does not end there. Since the board has defined the CEO's performance to be identical to organizational performance, the Operational Expectations and the Results policies are the performance standards for the CEO.

And if the board advances this concept one additional step and requires (in an OE policy) that every employee must be evaluated by the same method as the board evaluates the CEO (i.e., according to their compliance with the OE policies and their contribution toward achieving the Results policies), these policies become the standards for every employee's performance! This concept requires systemic alignment throughout the organization, from the boardroom to the boiler room.

It now should be obvious that in order for this interwoven set of standards to have any real meaning, all actual performance must be monitored against the standards. One of the policies in the Governance Culture section is an annual work plan for the board, an example of which may be found as table 9.1. One of the most important parts of that annual work plan is a schedule for monitoring each of these policies.

Remember, when all the policy development is complete, the board will have about thirty policies, total, divided into the four separate policy types we have discussed. Each one of them will be calendared for monitoring at some point during the year.

As the board monitors each policy, it is examining whether board, organizational, or individual performance has matched the standard. If so, celebrations break out! If not, strategies for closing the gaps become the discussion of the day, and the policy may be scheduled for re-monitoring by the board.

At the end of the year, nothing that goes on in the organization escapes formal and official monitoring.

SELF-MONITORING

As a rule, the board self-monitors each policy in the Governance Culture and the Board-CEO Relationship categories. The schedule for monitoring these policies is recorded in the board's annual work plan. The monitoring interval need not be one or more policies at each meeting; the board could self-monitor all of them once each year, or conduct self-monitoring mini-retreats each quarter, for example.

There are options to the self-monitoring process, however. Some of our clients have created external monitoring committees, composed of people outside the organization who are trained to observe the board in action and offer oral and written critiques of the board's performance. This is good only to a point, since some board and board member behaviors may not be observable in meetings.

The most effective GC and BCR monitoring processes are done in facilitated retreats, where members can talk openly and candidly about their observations of the board's and individual members' behavior and whether they meet the standards set in policy. Self-monitoring is difficult to do in a public business meeting, which is why we recommend doing it in a retreat setting. Even those meetings can be considered open meetings for some public boards, but the glare of the spotlight usually is less bright in such settings.

Table 9.1
PALM SPRINGS UNIFIED SCHOOL DISTRICT BOARD OF EDUCATION
POLICY TYPE: GOVERNANCE CULTURE
GC 6-E Annual Work Plan

Month	GC	BCR	OE	Results	Linkages	Board Development	Other Business
Jan	4, 5, 6, 10		3				Annual Retreat CEO Summative Evaluation Aspen (9-10) SSC
Feb			6 EX				NSBA/FRN
Mar			6				Adopt Policies 3/27
Apr		1-5 ('08)	2		KC (4-26)	Dealing w/sensitive issues	Aspen NSBA
May			10	2.1 – 2.6 (RI)			
June	1, 2, 3		1, 5	2.7 (RI)			Aspen 26&27 CEO Formative Evaluation
July			8				
Aug			11, 12				
Sept			7, 9	3 (RI & I)		Data Training	
Oct	7, 8, 9		13	4 (RI & I)		Budget	Aspen (23 & 24) Wisdom Sharing
Nov			4	2.1-2.6 (I & B)			
Dec			6	2.7 (I&B)			CSBA

Other potential board development topics: Media Skills; Conflict Resolution

RI: Reasonable Interpretation; I: Indicators; B: Baseline; M: Monitoring;

KC: Key Communicators

Identifying issues is the easy part; exploring solutions to close any identified performance gaps is the more difficult part.

But despite the difficulty, continuous improvement of board performance demands that this process of self-monitoring be taken seriously—at least as seriously as the monitoring of the policies in other parts of the model. We include as appendix A an example of a board's self-assessment summary.

MONITORING OPERATIONAL EXPECTATIONS POLICIES

In both Operational Expectations and Results policy monitoring, the board has a range of process options to consider. The board can monitor these policies by three methods, including:

- *Internal Report.* The internal report method is the one usually chosen by the board for monitoring each OE policy, since it requires no additional board time or money. Internal reports are prepared by the CEO (or a designated staff member) and submitted for the board's acceptance.

  Some board members initially may be tempted to assume that such reports cannot be trusted, since they are developed by the CEO and staff, who could not possibly be free of bias.

  We caution against such assumptions. Each internal report begins with the following statement from the CEO to the board: "I hereby certify that as of (date), the following represents a true and accurate statement of condition related to the provisions of Policy___." A CEO would be foolish to present false evidence to the board following such a signed certification of truthfulness.

  But equally significant, it is the obligation of the CEO to present a reasonable interpretation of the board's policy language, and solid evidence of compliance, acceptable to the board. The board itself assesses the adequacy of the evidence. If the board receives a report that it considers unreasonable or insufficient, it is not obligated to accept it.

  Remember, the organization's and the CEO's performance are the same. It is in the CEO's best interest to present reports that are complete, convincing in their strength, and adequate in themselves as evidence of organizational compliance in the area being monitored. Since these reports become the basis for the CEO's own evaluation, they are to be taken seriously.

- *External Report.* If the board chooses, it may select an outside party to assess on behalf of the board the organization's state of compliance. Boards essentially use an independent financial auditor for similar purposes (although most financial audits fail to examine financial conditions against policy provisions as a standard).

  If external reports are used, it is important that the examiner understand the provisions of the policy, since the policy is the performance standard, and the governing environment within which the work is being done.

  This option is not used as frequently as the internal report, since there usually is cost involved in having third-party monitoring work conducted. But if, for whatever reason, the board chooses to use the external report, it can do so in any policy area, not only finance.

- *Board Inspection.* The third option for monitoring organizational performance is board inspection. This option typically is used even less frequently, but it is available if the board feels the need.

  This method requires that the board, as an entity, decide to inspect conditions directly, and do so either as a full body or via the use of a board-approved committee charged to do that specific and well-defined work. It requires board time, but usually not much else.

  As was the case with external reporting, it is important that board inspections be based on the standards set by the policy being monitored, and not allowed to degenerate into organized witch hunts.

All of these methods are available to the board for Operational Expectations monitoring, but in our experience, the use of the internal report dominates as the method most often used.

It is not unusual for some boards and CEOs initially to assume that these new reporting requirements will consume their time and become an enormous burden that will dominate their lives. The process does require some serious work by staff, especially during the first year of reporting, but the process should eliminate a number of random, uncoordinated, and frequently unnecessary reports of various types. The best hope is that all such miscellaneous reports can find their way into the regularly scheduled monitoring process and be eliminated as stand-alone reports.

We are reminded of an incident from several years ago when a school superintendent initially was a reluctant player in the board's initial work in developing its policies and undergoing implementation training in monitoring. He went along for the ride, but he was not an enthusiastic passenger.

After about three cycles of monitoring reports, we received a message from him, announcing his full, complete, and enthusiastic support for this new process. Why? He observed that through this monitoring process, there is no part of the organization that is not deliberately and thoroughly opened up at least once each year for examination. Everything is evaluated on schedule, and if something isn't working, it will become obvious, he told us. And he was correct.

WHAT THE BOARD LOOKS FOR

When the board receives an OE monitoring report, it is looking for two things: whether the board's broad policy language has been reasonably interpreted and whether there is sufficient evidence to judge compliance. The board is not looking for perfection; it is looking for reasonable interpretation and compliance.

The board must embed this standard of reasonableness throughout. Perfection likely will never be achieved in the life of most organizations because bad things happen. The board is looking for whether they are aberrations, as well as how the CEO dealt with them.

Of course, deliberate policy violations or noncompliant conditions that are controllable by the CEO should never be tolerated. Some noncompliant conditions are less egregious than others, of course, so the board is expected to exercise reasonable judgment when monitoring organizational performance.

We include as appendix B an example of a board's Operational Expectations monitoring report.

MONITORING RESULTS

Effectively monitoring Results policies will be the last piece to fall into place, once a board begins implementation of Coherent Governance. This is true because the board is looking for two things when it monitors Results, one of which is not available at the outset.

First, as was the case with Operational Expectations policies, the board is looking for a reasonable interpretation of its policy language. That part can be provided during year one, but the second thing the board is looking for cannot: reasonable progress.

Let's take the Results monitoring sequence in a couple of steps. The reasonable interpretation component includes four subparts, all of which must be developed and approved by the board well before actual monitoring can occur. They are as follows:

- *Literal interpretation.* This is one of the most important parts of any monitoring report, because if the CEO and staff cannot offer an interpretation considered by the board to be reasonable, all the work that follows will be unreasonable as well. The challenge for the CEO is to state what he or she believes the board's underlying value was when it wrote the policy directive.

  If the board said, for example, that it expects every student to be literate, what does "literate" mean? Is it simply reading at grade level? Or does it require the ability to speak and write? What about higher-order use of words and thoughts? What about technological literacy? The interpretation is basic to all that follows.
- *Selection of indicators.* What bodies of evidence can the CEO and staff use to effectively demonstrate progress? If we use the example above, what tests or other kinds of evidence does the district have to allow it to assess whether students are literate?
- *Establish baseline performance.* Before any CEO can assert reasonable progress, he or she first must know the starting point. The above example again: where are kids performing now on each of the selected indicators? This baseline sets the stage for the fourth component of reasonable interpretation, which is:
- *Set short-term and long-term performance targets.*

If the CEO and staff have offered a reasonable interpretation and a reasonable choice of indicators, established their baselines, and set reasonable targets, the board should approve all these components during year one of implementation.

Why? Because once the board has approved all these initial components, the board and CEO are on the same page in terms of having defined what reasonable progress is and how it will be measured. There should be no debate about that.

At some future point, actual monitoring data will be presented, using data from the selected indicators, with progress compared with the baseline to indicate whether the targets were hit. If they were, there should be no debate; reasonable progress has been achieved.

But what if the targets were not achieved? What if the trend lines moved in the right direction, but targets were missed?

This is where reasonable, informed judgment must come into play. To some extent, that judgment must be tempered with knowledge of the industry the organization is in. If the organization is an industry that sells cars, the volume of sales and the resulting profit are fairly quantifiable and judgment may be fairly easy.

But if the industry is a public school district that serves kids, perhaps with high mobility and other factors at work, the judgment is much less precise. This is where reasonable people must exercise reasonable judgment in making the determination about whether reasonable progress has been made.

A lot of reasonables, we understand! But we know of no other way to make the judgment in an organization that deals with people as a product.

Effectively monitoring Results is the most difficult part of Coherent Governance implementation—but also the most important. If the organization exists to produce something of value for the owners and clients, this is where the action is.

This is the bottom line, the "profit substitute" that drives public and nonprofit organizations. There is no greater role a board can play than deciding what those benefits are, demanding that the organization successfully deliver them, and monitoring to assure that it does. Included as appendix C is an example of a Results monitoring report.

SUMMARY

The four quadrants of policy combine to form a set of standards for the performance of every part of the organization. The board self-assesses its performance in the Governance Culture and Board-CEO Relationship categories. The Operational Expectations and Results policies may be monitored via internal report, external report, or board inspection. The usual method is internal report. When the board monitors the OE and R policies, it is looking for a reasonable interpretation, compliance with the OE policies, and reasonable progress toward achieving the R policies.

QUESTIONS FOR THOUGHT

1. Does your board have standards for its own performance? How does it now monitor its performance?
2. Is your organization now operating in a manner consistent with the board's values? How do you know?
3. Is your organization now producing acceptable results for the owners and clients it serves? How do you know?

Systemic Application and Alignment

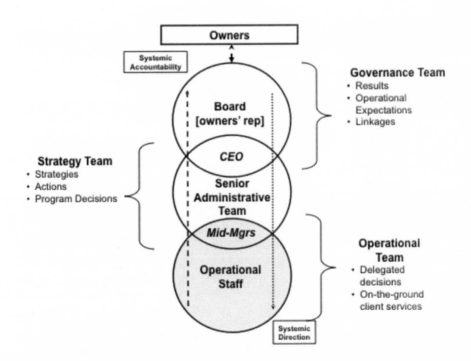

Creating a governing model to help the board do its work better makes sense as a stand-alone goal, but if the venture stopped there, a vast storehouse of organizational benefits would go unopened.

Earlier in this book, we talked about the fact that in many organizations, boards merely are tolerated, or worse. Many boards are ignored or "managed" by the organizations they theoretically lead. We all have seen it: staff actions are on autopilot. The board meets once a month or so—and the world may stop for a few hours while it does, only to resume its normal functioning immediately thereafter without regard for anything the board did.

Creating an effective governing system recognizes that the work of the board is important, not as a vehicle just to improve the board's performance, but one that drives everything that happens throughout the operational organization.

Figure 10.1, at the top of the previous page, illustrates how Coherent Governance can and should be applied as a vehicle to align the entire organization behind the direction provided by the board in policy.

Each of the three linked circles represents a team whose work is a key part of a coherent whole. At the top, the Governance Team, comprising the board and the CEO, is responsible for creating the organizational vision, for establishing the outcome goals or results the organization is expected to deliver for the owners and clients it serves, and for defining the standards of operational performance it expects. Of course, the board is the decision maker on the team, but the CEO is a key player as the board's chief advisor and the operational leader.

The work of the Governance Team drives action at every level of the organization, as represented by the vertical line on the right side of the diagram. The organizational results established by the board become the outcomes required of the organization. The operational standards become the performance targets for every division of the organization and for every employee.

As we stated earlier, the CEO is a member of the Governance Team, but he also has another role: the leader of the Strategy Team, comprising the key members of the CEO's senior staff or administrative cabinet, and even site-level leaders.

Once the Governance Team has set the performance expectations for the organization (the "whats"), the Strategy Team picks up the responsibility for designing the "hows," the strategies and actions necessary to make that vision a reality.

It is clear from the example that, as Coherent Governance is applied to organizational alignment, it naturally assigns the traditional components of strategic planning to the logical owners of those components: the board owns the organization's vision, mission, and goals (Results), while the staff owns the strategies and actions. The board, through its Results policies, sets the outcome expectations, and the staff is free to design strategies, actions, and programs to meet those expectations.

Mid-managers, who are members of the Strategy Team, also serve as the leaders of the third team, the Operational Team. This team is responsible for ground-level decisions, within their level of assigned authority, to achieve the outcomes and operational standards the board has set in policy.

In any organization, regardless of its size or complexity, this is where things either happen or not. In a school district, it matters little how well the board crafts Results policies, or how logical the district-wide strategies are, if nothing happens in the schools and classrooms to cause kids to achieve at higher levels.

This is precisely why complete organizational alignment and clear accountability become so crucial to the ultimate application of any governing system.

Notice the vertical line on the left side of the diagram. Through the monitoring process, systemic accountability for organizational performance flows from the operational level all the way back to the board. If any part of the operational organization fails to be held accountable for performance, the system has lost its integrity.

One additional fact should become clear from this diagram. We mentioned in an earlier chapter the flawed concept of teamwork displayed in some organizations, namely boards and CEOs both agreeing on every course of action—and confusing accountability in the process. In this diagram, each team is responsible for distinctly different decisions, and each is held accountable for the decisions it makes. Teams play complementary, but different, roles, and they perform them with controlled independence and full accountability. There never should be ambiguity about who makes which decision, or who is accountable for which outcome.

ONE COHERENT WHOLE

We referred earlier to Coherent Governance as an operating system for boards. By definition, a system means a set of connected things or parts forming a complex whole, or a set of parts working together in an interconnected network. What, then, is included in this governing system for boards? What would a board expect to have as a result of adopting this way of doing business?

- *A new set of governing policies*, which collectively set performance standards for the board, the organization, and the CEO. The new policies would be distinct from the board's large and typically unwieldy policies, which usually become operational policies and are assigned to the CEO for daily administrative use.
- *The components of an organizational strategic plan* owned by the board: Mission/Vision and Goals (Results); the "whats," with the "hows" (Strategies and Actions) delegated to the CEO and staff.
- *A meaningful board self-assessment process*, all built around the board's self-determined performance standards, as defined in the Governance Culture and Board-CEO Relationship policies.
- *An authentic and performance-based CEO evaluation process and format.* Since the organization's performance and the CEO's performance are the same, the board's monitoring of the Results and Operational Expectations policies creates a "portfolio" of organizational performance, which is transferred to the CEO at the end of the cycle.
- *A full-year calendar* scheduling board focus and work, which will drive board meeting agendas for the next twelve months.
- *A credible board job description* to focus the board on its role of serving, representing, and leading the ownership.
- *A CEO job description* that doesn't end with "other duties as assigned."
- *A process for clearly and rigorously evaluating the performance of every element of the organization's operation.* The Operational Expectations monitoring activities allow no part of the organization's performance to be ignored.
- *A process for evaluating the effectiveness of the organization's efforts to serve its owners and clients.* Monitoring Results policies assures the board that its defined outcomes for clients and owners are being provided.
- *A framework for building a communication link* between the board and its owners and stakeholders. This is relationship building to sustain the organization as it works to achieve outcomes.

All of these components are encompassed in a single, coherent system. Boards typically have developed such systems and processes independently, with the result being a set of uncoordinated and disconnected parts that may or may not work together.

SUMMARY
The application of Coherent Governance creates alignment of the organization's functions, from the boardroom throughout the operational side of the organization. Three interconnected teams have separate authority and responsibility for various functions, and each is fully accountable for the decisions it makes.

Coherent Governance is a coordinated system that includes a number of features that boards typically create in separate, uncoordinated ventures. The end result is that each component fits within an overall framework and results in complete organizational alignment. Coherent Governance achieves systemic, systematic, and sustainable leadership for any organization that seeks to achieve excellence.

QUESTIONS FOR THOUGHT
1. How would you describe your organization's alignment, beginning with the board and extending throughout the operational organization?
2. How much of what happens in your organization is driven by the board and its vision for organizational performance?
3. Does your board now have a coordinated system for getting its work done?

11

Governing Coherently

How Can a Board Transform Itself?

A number of years ago, a senior director in one of our client organizations commented to us: "Implementing this thing isn't easy."

He was right. A board's willingness to practice Coherent Governance, including its intensive work to develop sound policies, its serious attention to implementation training and coaching, and its formal adoption of the model, do not in themselves assure successful implementation.

In our careers, we have seen far more successes than failures, but failure can—and unfortunately does—occur. What causes failure? And what are the ingredients necessary to assure successful implementation and, equally important, long-term sustainability?

We have given the issue serious thought during the past few years and have tried to assess the factors that seem to be critical to both short-term and long-term success. We have observed both positive and negative factors that seem to determine whether a board can achieve the level of excellence that the governance model promises.

These are the positive conditions that we believe contribute to success. The antitheses of these conditions are easily identified as factors that can diminish the likelihood of any board's success—hopefully not your own board's!

So just what are the apparent ingredients that combine to produce excellent governing? These are clear to us:

- *Genuine commitment of the board.* As obvious as this appears, it isn't always present. Some boards are intrigued with the idea of doing something new and different, of being seen as a trailblazer, but are less than fully committed to actually doing the work to achieve it.

  Adopting a complete new and different governing model isn't the same as playing with a shiny new toy, which invariably grows old after a time. Commitment means learning new behaviors, and exercising self and group discipline to remain "model consistent" as you govern in a new way. It means resisting the temptation to blame the model when the first challenge hits—as it surely will.

  Commitment to and nurturing confidence in the model provide the sturdy and basic foundation for effective implementation and achieving excellent results for the organization as it weathers challenges and change over the long term.

- *The board's willingness to change old behaviors.* It should be clear that adopting a completely new and different way of doing business requires old habits and customs to change. Easy to say and always harder to do.

  Earlier we challenged boards to consider that this is the very first meeting of this board; it has no history. If the board had such a luxury, how would it choose to structure how it gets work done? Would it rebuild a culture exactly like the one it has been practicing, or would it create a completely fresh one, unencumbered with history and tradition—*the way we've always done it?*

  We are not saying that every past practice is unworthy, but rather suggesting that a board must be willing to free itself from past practice and create a culture that is based upon thoughtful exploration of what is possible, not what it is comfortable with. It is a call for WSOD—a *willing suspension of disbelief*—as you let go of the ring and fly up to the next level of performance. It calls for historical appreciation, but not living in history.

- *Recognition that a new governing model will not automatically solve all old problems.* Occasionally we have been invited to work with a board that is so dysfunctional that anything that floats by appears to be a life preserver. Sometimes boards find themselves in such distress that they are tempted to adopt the view that if they can just adopt Coherent Governance, all their internal problems will go away.

Typically, the problems they are dealing with are people problems, not structural problems: lack of trust, poor communication, a history of divisive behaviors. It is true that adopting a sound operating system can provide the structure to help boards deal with the tough people problems. Governance Culture and Board-CEO Relationship policies are designed to do just that. But until such dysfunctional conditions are addressed, no governing system in itself will make life good again for such boards.

- *Boards must have patience.* Changing to a new way of getting work done requires time and practice. When we work with boards, we frequently ask members to write their names on a pad. Then we ask them to place the pen in their opposite hand, and do it again. Then we analyze what they experienced.

They typically say that the second time was slower, messier, awkward, required more attention and thought. In general, the non-preferred hand was less efficient with a less-desirable, even childish outcome.

Implementing a new governing model can be that way too. In order to become a mature Coherent Governance board, to gain efficiency and achieve the desired outcome, new behaviors must be learned and new skills developed. This requires time, practice, and patience.

This is why we strongly encourage boards to maintain an extended coaching relationship, providing an outside "eye" to identify, address, and facilitate improvement for the board, its members, and staff, whose working life will change, just as will the board's. Remember, even champions need coaching!

- *A CEO who is confident in his own abilities, willing to assume accountability for independent actions, and supportive of the board's new role.* Some CEOs say they support the board's venture into a governing model that requires them to exercise independent leadership and be held accountable for it, but then they continue to seek board approvals for decisions that are now theirs to make—reacting either out of fear or tradition.

Some CEOs openly resist the board's new level of governing leadership and policy-level control, and set up roadblocks of infinite types. Some go into this work thinking it will "control" the board, only to discover that the board simultaneously can become more active in exercising control but less intrusive with micromanagement. Others may be unwilling to change their own administrative behaviors to align the organization with the board's governing culture.

When a board adopts Coherent Governance, it changes not only its own way of doing business, but maybe equally dramatically, it changes the way the organization does its work. If a CEO either is unwilling or incapable of transforming the organization as necessary to support the board, the board's good work can be painfully slow or jeopardized.

Coherent Governance can be the most freeing environment imaginable for the skilled, confident CEO. But it can be oil on water for a CEO who lacks confidence and competence to do the job free of board approvals, or who is resistant to assuming accountability for results.

- *Support necessary to allow the board to succeed.* Adopting a new governing model requires more support for board processes than the old system required. The board must have staff support to assure rigorous, accurate, and on-time monitoring records; to maintain the annual work plan; and to manage the logistics of a linkage or owner engagement plan.
- *A board's willingness to deal effectively with the outliers.* When we first started this work, we had a company policy that required a board to agree unanimously to pursue the governing model. We later relaxed that requirement, moving to a requirement for a "critical mass" in order to prevent a single member from determining the future of the entire board.

Nevertheless, even a single outlier can distract the board, and attention must be paid to those members who may not be in sync with the board majority. They come in all forms, ranging from willing but not enthusiastic, to true skeptics, to declared opponents, to outright saboteurs.

Those who are willing to join the board majority and try to make it work, despite some reservations, usually come on board. Their views are important and must be heard. Over time, there is a good chance that the board's success will elevate their level of support.

It is the saboteurs who concern us. These are the members who not only oppose what the majority is doing, but also try to assure that the whole venture fails. Their overt behaviors can take several forms, but you know them by their actions.

A board cannot allow individual members to divert its attention or waste its time, nor can it allow the destructive agendas of a single member, or a distinct minority, to determine the board's fate. We still govern in a democracy, by majority rule. A number of possible remedies are available to the board to help deal with destructive behaviors, and those must be used as the board continues to seek to build unity and focus.

- *Recognition that the model is a means, not the end.* Adopting a new governance operating system is an important step for any board. At the beginning, there are new processes and behaviors to learn, and it takes careful attention by the members to learn how to use the new tools available to the board.

    But we have seen boards become so consumed with "getting it right" that they became slaves to the model, rather than using the model as a way to get board work done. There is a high level of discipline required of a board in order to live with the commitments it has made in policy. That said, within a reasonable period of time, the board and staff should be comfortable with this operating system as their adopted platform and practice using it to focus on achieving Results.

There are a number of other conditions that contribute to a board's likely success in implementing Coherent Governance, but these we have observed as critical. If any one of them is not present, the board labors under a major disadvantage as it tries to make the transition.

Building a new governance culture and executing systematic, systemic, and accountable leadership to make a difference for those you serve is difficult, even when all the stars line up just right. To achieve sustainable governing excellence, to fulfill your hope and promise for leadership, it is critical to self-assess against these criteria and find the way to resolve crippling issues.

Taking this journey is an exciting venture, an opportunity to literally transform not only the board, but every part of the organization for which the board is responsible. The first step always is the biggest one. But taking it, and making the conscious choice for good governance, can be the greatest legacy a board can leave for those members who follow.

Appendix A: Board Self-Assessment

GC-7 ANNUAL BOARD PLANNING CYCLE

GC MONITORING REPORT
(This board's self-assessment language response is in italics.)
To accomplish its work with a governance style consistent with board policies, the board will follow an annual agenda that (a) completes a survey of Results policies at least biannually, (b) strives to improve its performance through attention to board education and enriched input and deliberation, and (c) completes the monitoring of Operational Expectations policies, Governance Culture policies, and Board-CEO Relationship policies.

1. The cycle will conclude each year on the last day of March in order that administrative decisions and budgeting can be based on accomplishing the current board policies.
   In compliance. This year's monitoring cycle begins with our April 8th meeting and will end with the last meeting in March.
   In the first two months of the new cycle, the board will develop its agenda for the ensuing one-year period.
   In compliance. The board will have on its agenda for the first meeting in May to adopt the new annual board calendar for the coming year.

2. Education, input, and deliberation will receive paramount attention in structuring board meetings and other board activities during the year.

Not in Compliance. The board has received its first Results monitoring reports in three areas. There has been considerable effort made to allow for the majority of time to be spent evaluating and discussing these reports.

However, there have been two issues this year that have been in front of the board for an excessive amount of time and have taken away from the board's priority function, to address Results for our clients.

Commitment to Improve: As a result of the excess time spent on these issues, the board will look at its procedure for having items on its agenda for reconsideration. The board did reconstruct its form for "Audience Comments" in an effort to be more efficient when it receives input from the community.

Approved: Date:

Appendix B: Operational Expectations Monitoring Report

RACINE UNIFIED SCHOOL DISTRICT OPERATIONAL EXPECTATIONS MONITORING REPORT

OE-10 (INSTRUCTIONAL PROGRAM)

SUMMARY OF COMPLIANCE STATUS

Date:

Superintendent Certification:

With respect to Operational Expectation 10 (Instructional Program), the superintendent certifies that the proceeding information is accurate and complete, and is:

_____ In Compliance

___X___ In Compliance, with Exceptions (as noted in the evidence)

_____ Not in Compliance

Signed: _____ Date:_____

Superintendent

Board of Education Action:

With respect to Operational Expectation 10 (Instructional Program), the Board:

_____ Accepts the report as fully compliant

_____ Accepts the report as compliant with noted exceptions

_____ Finds the report to be noncompliant

Summary statement/motion of the Board:

_____

_____

_____

_____

Signed:_____ Date: _____

Board President

> The superintendent shall maintain a program of instruction that offers challenging and relevant opportunities for all students to achieve at levels defined in the board's Results policies.
> The superintendent will:

Interpretation:

The board values that the program used to teach students is demanding and stimulating, designed to push students to higher levels of achievement in pursuit specifically of the board's stated values for student achievement in the Results policies.

The board values an instructional program that is designed based on the best practices in the areas of curriculum, instruction, assessment, and social interaction. Our interpretation for each of these components is below. The Teaching and Learning Framework provides a structure for organizing these big ideas around student learning. We interpret:

- Curriculum is the knowledge, content, and skills that are written, taught, and assessed. The curriculum is based on state standards that are broken down into learning targets at each grade and subject level. Enduring understandings or big rocks are identified as essential ideas to be learned. Essential or guiding questions help to focus student learning on the enduring understandings.
- Instruction is the methodology used to convey the curriculum.
- Assessment has two major components: formative and summative. The purpose of formative assessment is to check for students' understanding and adjust instruction accordingly. Summative assessment is designed to formally assess what students know and are able to do.
- Social interaction recognizes that all learning is constructed through experiences and interaction with peers, teachers, and the environment.

10.1 Ensure that instructional programs are based on a comprehensive and objective review of best practices research.	Compliant

Interpretation:
The board values an instructional program that is developed with full awareness of the work and practices of current research, other districts' practice, and educators. Further, it values that the study of other works is to be done without bias—allowing for full review and openness to bring those practices to our district.

Evidence of Compliance:
According to the National Research Council's publication, *How People Learn* (2000), and additional research by Zemel, Daniels, and Hyde's *Best Practice: Today's Standards for Teaching and Learning in America's Schools* (2005), best practices in education can be divided into four major categories:

1. Student-centered: students learn best when the material is relevant to their lives. Learning activities must be challenging, yet attainable. Hands-on and active learning are the most powerful forms of learning.

2. Cognitive: activities that focus on higher-order thinking skills for all students are essential. Students must create or re-create meaning using all modes of learning.
3. Social: learning is experience-based. Students must be given opportunities to interact with one another and their teachers in a manner that creates opportunities for success.
4. Knowledge-based: experts organize problems differently from novice learners. Deep understanding of content-based issues is a hallmark of a knowledge-based learner.

As part of the district effort to bring coherence to a vision for Teaching and Learning, a framework was adopted that incorporates the elements described above. This framework incorporates work by Grant Wiggins and Jay McTighe's *Understanding by Design* and the Instructional Process initiative into Racine's Teaching and Learning Framework.

As new research is published, current practices are evaluated and amended. Continuous Progress, used for the elementary reading, has been modified to retain the essential tenet that students are taught at the appropriate instructional level, while exposing students to grade-level knowledge, concepts, and skills through differentiated instruction.

As the curriculum section of the instructional management system, SchoolNet, is developed this summer, a comprehensive repository for the instructional program will be accessible to all staff and parents. The framework will be included in the SchoolNet software as a way to structure curriculum, assessment, and instruction. Professional development to deepen understanding of this model is in the planning stages and will be introduced at the Shared Leadership Academy. This work will begin this summer and be updated on a yearly basis.

10.2	Base instruction on academic standards that meet or exceed state and/or nationally recognized model standards.	Compliant

Interpretation:

We interpret "base instruction" to mean the district's core instructional program that all students receive.

We interpret "meet or exceed state and/or nationally recognized model standards" to mean that the district's instructional program is based on the Wisconsin State Model Academic Standards.

The board values district curriculum and instructional programs designed to meet levels approved by the federal government—assuring our program is competitive with other districts throughout the state. As a result, the board of education adopted state standards as the district's local standards, as well. Curriculum guides are written to correlate with the Wisconsin State Model Academic Standards.

Evidence of Compliance:

The Wisconsin Model Academic Standards are the basis for district curriculum writing projects. The state standards are based on national standards developed by national and international organizations (e.g., International Reading Association, National Council for Teachers of Math, etc.).

Research that is supported by these various organizations and others is the foundation for the Wisconsin Model Academic Standards. Currently, the district is breaking down the state standards by grade and subject area to provide teachers with clear subject and grade level targets. This work is completed in the following grade levels and subject areas:

- Mathematics, grades K–8
- English Language Arts, grades K–8
- Social Studies, grades K–12
- Physical Education, grades K–12
- Career and Technology Education

This summer, the following subject areas and grade levels will be complete:

- Science, grades K–12
- Mathematics, grades 9–12
- English, grades 9–12

As stated in 10.1, this work will be available to staff and parents via SchoolNet. Professional development will be structured around this framework and its components as well.

10.3 Align curriculum with the standards.	Compliant

Interpretation:
The board values that what we teach students is directly relating to the achievement of the adopted state and local standards.

We interpret "align curriculum" to mean that instruction is based on the Wisconsin State Model Academic Standards and that the content, knowledge, skills, assessments, and the selection of materials are based on these standards.

Evidence of Compliance:
During the summer, curriculum and instruction coordinators and supervisors with teams of teachers develop curriculum guides. Curriculum guides link units of instruction to the Wisconsin standards.

Capacity Building:
These guides exist for all core academic areas and many elective areas.
Summer curriculum writing will include rewrites and updates for the following courses:

- English 11
- CP Geometry
- Health 9
- Elementary Physical Education
- U.S. History
- AP World History
- Science, grades 6–8
- Science, grade 9

10.4 Effectively measure each student's progress toward achieving or exceeding the standards.	Compliant

Interpretation:
The board values that all students' work is evaluated with reliability and validity against their progress toward or surpassing identified standards.

We interpret "effectively measure" to mean that the district uses formative and summative assessment tools to determine students' progress in achieving the North Star vision. More specifically, the summative assessment tools include the Wisconsin Knowledge and Concepts Exams (WKCE). The formative assessment tools include the Northwestern Evaluation Association's Measures of Academic Progress (NWEA MAP).

Evidence of Compliance:
The district measures student process against the state standards in core academic areas using the Wisconsin Knowledge and Concepts Exams (WKCE), which are aligned to the Wisconsin state standards. Several core academic content areas have begun to create common formative and summative assessment measures to further increase knowledge regarding student progress. Additionally, the district also measures student progress in reading and mathematics three times a year in grades 2–9 using the Measures of Academic Progress.

Capacity Building:
Although we can effectively measure student progress and have processes in place to do so, staff access to these data can be cumbersome and difficult. The Instructional Management System, SchoolNet, will house the assessments mentioned above. This will provide staff and our parents/guardians easy access to student achievement data that can be used to drive instruction. These data will be loaded prior to the August 9 Shared Leadership Data Retreat.

10.5 Ensure that the instructional program includes opportunities for students to develop talents and interests in more specialized areas.	Compliant

Interpretation:
The board values that the district program offers students the ability to pursue and achieve in fields that they either have identified aptitude for or for which they have particular affinity.

We interpret "more specialized areas" to include the arts, music, and career and technology education fields, and specialized curricular offerings such as the International Baccalaureate program.

Evidence of Compliance:
RUSD offers a very wide variety of program opportunities in specialized areas including career and technology education, the arts, music, Advanced Placement, International Baccalaureate, and dual enrollment programs.

Approximately 16 percent of RUSD students successfully complete a career and technology education program that results in a state certificate. The arts and music programs continue to strive in the face of reduced resources. There has been an increase in the number of students taking AP and IB courses in the past three years, as well as an increase in the number of courses offered. Two schools, Jefferson Elementary and McKinley Middle School, are currently in the process of becoming IB schools. Case High School expanded the number of IB course offerings in the area of mathematics this year.

10.6 Ensure that the instructional program addresses the different learning styles and needs of students of various backgrounds and abilities.	Compliant

Interpretation:
The board values that district offerings, instructional materials, and teaching approaches and styles accommodate different learning styles.

We interpret different learning styles to include: auditory, sensory, kinesthetic, and varying requirements of individual students who arrive at school with different physical, psychological, emotional, and cognitive needs and even lagging development, disability, or cultural and language barriers.

Evidence of Compliance:
Currently, RUSD has specialized instructional programs for struggling and advanced learners. The diverse learning needs of students can be met either through specialized instructional programs (Advanced Placement or Read 180), through differentiated instruction, or through the presence of charter, magnet, and choice schools. In Read 180, 597 students are enrolled at the

middle school level, and 155 students at the high school level. The number of students who take the Advanced Placement or International Baccalaureate courses for college credit has doubled since 2007.

Magnet schools, such as Jefferson, Red Apple, and Fine Arts Elementary are very popular options for families with students demonstrating an aptitude in the arts or with a gifted and talented designation. As evidenced by no parental complaint or due process hearings, all schools are in compliance with Standard (t), which stipulates that all schools will provide programming for students identified as gifted and talented.

Capacity Building:
The district is also exploring professional development options to increase capacity for differentiated instruction at all educational levels. Professional development in the area of differentiated instruction will be incorporated into the North Star Framework for Teaching and Learning.

10.7 Encourage new and innovative programs, carefully monitoring and evaluating the effectiveness of all such programs at least annually.	Noncompliant

Interpretation:
The board values new and innovative programs that align with the North Star vision and the board's Results policies. The District-Wide School Improvement Council (DWSIC) has developed a rubric to determine whether or not an improvement idea should be recommended to the cabinet for implementation.

We interpret "new and innovative programs" to be programs that are aligned to the North Star and provide alternate pathways to success.

We interpret "carefully monitoring and evaluating effectiveness" to mean that the identified success metrics for each program are reviewed on a yearly basis.

Evidence of Compliance:
The DWSIC thoroughly screens innovative ideas in relation to North Star goals prior to implementation. A self-assessment rubric exists for all schools to utilize for improvement ideas that do not reach a set monetary or resource threshold.

Individual schools received data at last year's Data Retreat that aided in the work around evaluating new programs. This process needs to become more intentional to assert compliance.

Capacity Building:
More work is needed in the area of program evaluation. As the DWSIC process continues to be used and institutionalized, program evaluation will be more a part of district culture. After the implementation of the instructional management system/data warehouse, longitudinal data will be more easily accessible to conduct program evaluation.

10.8 Ensure that all instructional programs, including both content and practice, are regularly evaluated and modified as necessary to assure their continuing effectiveness.	Compliant

Interpretation:
The board values that all curriculum and its teacher delivery are planned for systematic review on how well they are achieving the North Star and board's Results policies and that any deficiencies are addressed for improvement.

The board values the use of data analysis and school improvement plans that are based on these data. This information is essential to develop effective instructional programs.

We interpret "all instructional programs" to include the instruction received by all students in all subject and grade areas.

We interpret "regularly evaluated and modified" to mean that the district looks at student performance and classroom-level instructional changes occur.

Evidence of Compliance:
At last summer's data retreat, 285 teachers, staff members, and principals constituted building teams that analyzed the current level of student achievement and began the process of creating collaborative school improvement plans that are aligned to the North Star vision. The improvement plans specified classroom modifications needed to meet students' needs. The col-

laborative construction of the improvement plans assisted in their successful implementation and improved student achievement results on the WKCE given in November 2009.

10.9 Protect the instructional time provided for students during the academic day by prohibiting interruptions due to unnecessary intrusions, unnecessary teacher time out of the classroom, or the scheduling of activities that can be scheduled during other times.	Compliant

Interpretation:
The board values providing maximized time on task for student instruction and teacher-student contact time.

We interpret "protect the instructional time" to mean that the time a teacher is pulled away from the classroom for nonessential meetings and in-services is kept to a minimum.

We interpret "scheduled during other times" to include summer hours, after-school meetings, and utilization of early release time.

Evidence of Compliance:
The number of teachers who were excused from teaching duties to attend professional development activities was greatly reduced this year due to the implementation of a professional development calendar. Several larger professional development activities, such as the Shared Leadership Academy, were scheduled during the summer to prevent disruptions to classroom instruction. The district is also utilizing the Chiwaukee Academy to provide summer opportunities for professional development that are linked to new curriculum and textbook adoptions. These practices have drastically reduced the number of teacher absences that were not filled by a substitute teacher this year.

Building teams are utilizing early release time to reach consensus on school improvement plans and provide professional development surrounding these plans. Online surveys conducted after the first three early releases of the school year indicate that the vast majority of schools used this time for these activities.

10.10 Assure that the district calendar and the time made available during the instructional day assign priority to and best serve the learning needs of students.	Compliant

Interpretation:
The board values a calendar for students that provides longer instructional blocks without one- or two-day weeks. The calendar that has been developed follows traditional patterns. Efforts should be made to ensure that calendars are consistent with known standards of best instructional practices.

Evidence of Compliance:
The district calendar is a contractual item. Efforts were made to provide longer instructional blocks with more time for teachers to engage in collaborative learning.

10.11 Select textbooks and instructional materials that advance the achievement of the board's Results policies and that achieve continuity, integration, and articulation of the curriculum by course and program.	Compliant

Interpretation:
We interpret "select textbooks and instructional materials that advance achievement" to mean that the textbook adoption process follows the procedures specified in the DWSIC Handbook, as well as Croft Policy.

We interpret "achieve continuity, integration, and articulation of the curriculum by course and program" to mean that textbooks and instructional materials are selected based upon the curricular goals of the course.

Evidence of Compliance:

The content area coordinators and supervisors conduct all textbook adoption committees in accordance with the provisions outlined in the above documents. In addition, current best practice information is incorporated in the selection criteria for textbook materials. Best practice and curricular goals are used as criteria for selection of textbooks using the Tregoe process. Best practice informs the criteria for selection used by the adoption committees. A subcommittee of the DWSIC reviews the processes followed by all textbook committees. The chairperson of the DWSIC keeps documentation of this process. This year, the following courses and subjects underwent this process and were recommended to the Cabinet by the DWSIC for purchase:

- Middle School Keyboarding
- Keyboarding and Computer Applications
- Word Processing
- Computer Literacy
- Computer Applications
- Business and Personal Finance
- Marketing
- Accounting
- Advanced Accounting
- Family Living
- Construction
- Exploring Foods
- Power Systems
- Electronics
- Machine Fabrication
- French 3 and 4
- Elementary Spanish
- IB Math
- Elementary Math
- CP Geometry
- IB and AP Physics
- IB Chemistry
- 9 Lab Science
- Middle School Science

- Instrumental Music
- High School English
- Health

10.12 Regularly evaluate materials and textbooks, and maintain a procedure for reviewing such materials upon formal request by a parent or other stakeholder.	Compliant

Interpretation:

The board values a systematic approach to the selection and purchase of instructional materials and textbooks.

We interpret "regularly evaluate materials and textbooks" to mean that the district follows the board's policy of a nine-year adoption cycle or sooner depending upon extenuating circumstances.

We interpret "maintain a procedure for reviewing such materials upon formal request" to mean that textbook and classroom materials are available for public review upon request.

Evidence of Compliance:

The textbook adoptions cited in 10.11 were either at the end of their nine-year cycle or in the case of the Career and Technology Education courses were obsolete due to advances in technology. The College Board requires the AP Physics course to use a prescribed textbook to maintain status as an Advanced Placement course.

All textbook materials are available upon request from the corresponding curriculum and instruction coordinator or supervisor. All documentation for textbook selection is kept in the DWSIC minutes and is on file in the office of the director for curriculum and instruction.

10.13 Adequately monitor and control student access to and utilization of electronically distributed information.	Compliant

Interpretation:
The board values a process that ensures an adequate acceptable use policy has been established and the appropriate filters and monitoring mechanisms have been put in place by the district's information services department for employees and students.

Evidence of Compliance:
Currently, all students receive an Internet Usage Agreement form at the start of the school year. Parents and guardians may opt their student out of Internet usage by request. These agreements are kept on file at each school location. Teaching and Learning Department, Information Systems, and the Racine Educators' Association are collaboratively problem-solving issues relating to the implementation of Croft Policy that specifies the board's preference is toward less restrictive informational access.

10.14 Ensure appropriate input from students, parents, teachers, administrators, and other staff members involved in the instructional program as textbooks are reviewed and selected.	Compliant

Interpretation:
The board values a process that ensures methods are provided for all stakeholders to have appropriate input in textbook decisions.

Evidence of Compliance:
This year's textbook adoptions included administrators, teachers, parents, students, and a professor from a local university. The lists of textbook committee members are included in the documentation kept by the Director of Curriculum and Instruction. "Collaboration among all stakeholders" is one of five essential criteria developed by the DWSIC to evaluate the thoroughness of all recommended textbook materials. Documentation used by the DWSIC is attached.

Interpretation:
The board values a process in which annual reviews occur to assure that the enrollment in schools is fair and equitable based on building capacity.

| | Point Scale | | | | |
Criteria	4 (Superior)	3 (Adequate)	2 (Marginally Adequate)	1 (More work needed)	Score
Collaboration among Stakeholders	Clear documentary evidence that there was extensive and well-coordinated collaboration among stakeholders.	Clear documentary evidence that there was collaboration among stakeholders.	Some documentary evidence of collaboration.	Little or no evidence of collaboration.	
Explanation of Need for Improvement Action	Statements in final report clearly establish a compelling need for the improvement action and address urgency for the district.	Statements in final report clearly establish a need for the improvement action.	There is a statement of need; however, it is vague and unclear.	Little or no explanation of need is provided.	
Alignment with North Star	Statements in final report clearly relate to North Star and clearly target a specific area of improvement.	Statements in final report clearly address one or more areas of North Star.	There is limited indication of the relationship to North Star.	Little or no indication is provided as to the relationship to North Star.	
Research-Based Motivation for Improvement Action	Exemplary scholarship as demonstrated through comprehensive citations of recent scientific /evidence-based research and/ or other body of well-established information.	Scholarship as demonstrated through citation of recent scientific/evidence-based research and/ or other body of well-established information.	Limited evidence that the recommendation is based on recent research and/or other body of well-established information.	Little or no evidence that the recommendation is motivated by research and/ or other body of well-established information.	
Plan for Data Driven Methodology	Substantial and appropriate data are reported. Statements in final report provide detailed account of improvement action metrics.	Appropriate data have been collected. Statements in final report provide some detail as to improvement action metrics.	Limited data have been collected. Statements provide little detail as to improvement action metrics.	Little or no data have been collected. Few or no statements are made as to improvement action metrics.	

10.15 Review school attendance boundaries annually to assure reasonable balance in student enrollment, including recommendations for any school additions or closings.	Compliant

We interpret "to assure reasonable balance in student enrollment" to mean that the district will balance the physical capacity of the school building while reducing the number of students who are displaced from schools due to class size requirements for SAGE and P-5.

Evidence of Compliance:
Area superintendents monitor the school enrollment in September and April. The September monitoring occurs after the first couple of weeks of school. Adjustments in student enrollment based on building capacity are made at this time. This process is also monitored during April of the previous school year through the enrollment and staffing process that is conducted at each building.

The number of displaced students was greatly reduced this year due to a series of meetings held in late August and requests for waivers from DPI to keep as many students in their home schools as possible.

10.16 Provide guidelines and direction to staff regarding the teaching of controversial issues.	Compliant

Interpretation:
The board values a process that clearly articulates procedures regarding the teaching of controversial issues.

We interpret "controversial issues" to be any subject matter that elicits raised emotions due to local or world events.

Evidence of Compliance:
Guidelines exist in Croft Policy/Administrative Regulations regarding the teaching of controversial issues. This policy was e-mailed to social studies

department chairs after the vote on national health care and the subsequent charged discourse at the national level that followed. The district received no parental complaints following this episode.

The superintendent may not: 10.17 Change the basic grade configuration of district schools.	Compliant

Interpretation:
The board values a process that does not allow the superintendent to change the grade configurations without board approval.

We interpret the "basic grade configuration" to mean that the current PK–5, 6–8, and 9–12 composition of district schools may not be altered without board approval.

Evidence of Compliance:
Although this possibility has been discussed as part of the redistricting plan, no change has occurred.

The superintendent may not: 10.18 Change school attendance boundaries for students.	Compliant

Interpretation:
The board values its authority in deciding any alteration or reconfiguration of lines drawn for student attendance at school. The superintendent is prohibited from making such decisions.

The board values a process that does not allow school attendance boundaries to change without board approval.

Evidence of Compliance:
A Reinvesting Committee has been formed and made preliminary recommendations to the board. Only through this process will attendance boundaries change.

Appendix C: Results Monitoring Report

EDEN PRAIRIE PUBLIC SCHOOLS

RESULTS POLICY R-4—LIFE SKILLS

PURPOSE OF REPORT: APPROVAL OF INDICATORS, BASELINE, AND TARGET

REASONABLE INTERPRETATION APPROVED

Criteria for Board Review: Results Policies

1. The policy has been reasonably interpreted.
2. The organization is making reasonable progress toward achieving the board's stated results.
3. The information is sufficient to allow the board to decide.
4. The board will be looking for performance over time, trend lines moving in the right direction, steps that are being taken to improve, and reasons why improvement is or is not occurring.

Certification of the CEO: I certify this report to be accurate.
Date:

Melissa Krull

CEO

Policy: Students will live healthy, satisfying, and productive lives.

Interpretation:
Students will: demonstrate productive living through healthy and safe life choices, self-confidence, effectively working with others in both partnership and in relationship with others in authority, self-sufficiency in their own learning and talents, time management, and contribute to the good of others.

4.1   Understand and apply the principles of sound physical, mental, and emotional health.

Interpretation:
We interpret "understand and apply principles of sound physical, mental, and emotional health to mean that students will have knowledge and vocabulary of the basics of healthy living (wellness), will engage in group and individual activities (Interpersonal Skills), and demonstrate these principles through their actions.

"Apply the principles of sound physical health" means that students gain an understanding of how their bodies maintain health and understand implications of behaviors that impact that wellness.

"Apply the principles of sound mental and emotional health" means that students will understand their psychological well-being and use their cognitive and emotional capabilities to function in society, adjust to the recurrent stresses, and meet the ordinary demands of everyday life.

Revised: [date]

Indicators: Student self-report on substance use and risky behavior

Minnesota Student Survey—Eden Prairie Data, [date]

Baseline:

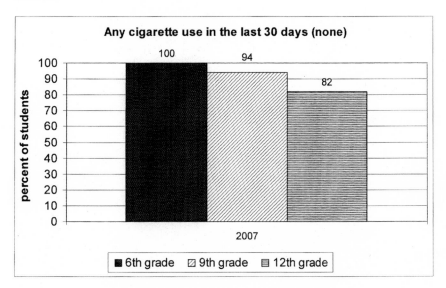

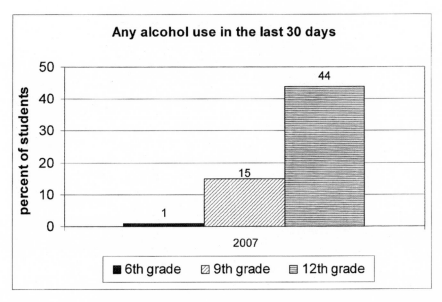

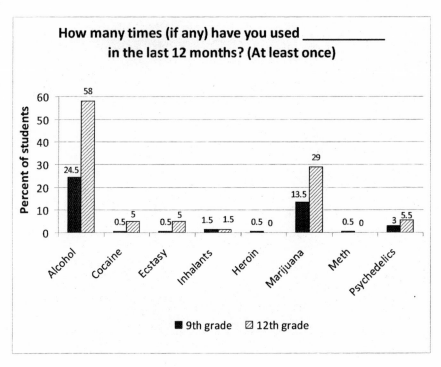

How many times (if any) have you used _____ in the last 12 months? (At least once)

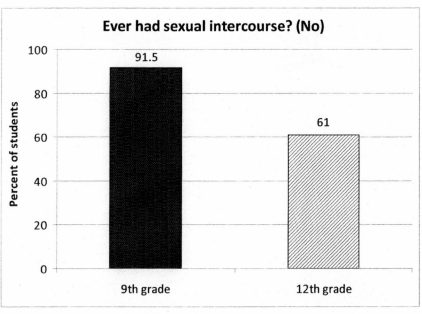

Ever had sexual intercourse? (No)

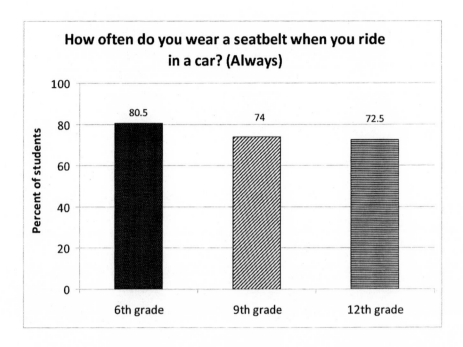

How often do you wear a seatbelt when you ride in a car? (Always)

Baseline Analysis: As students get older they demonstrate a steady increase in attempting what we would consider "unsafe" actions. It is evident that the area of greatest concern is the increase in alcohol use by the time a student is a senior.

4.2   Develop practical life skills to support self-sufficiency, including but not limited to:

- strong problem solving and critical thinking,
- work habits and ethics,
- time management, and
- personal financial competency.

Interpretation:

We interpret "practical life skills, strong problem solving, critical thinking, work habits and ethics, time management, and personal financial competency" to mean students who are independent, able to take care of themselves by thinking through challenges and resolving them, practicing acceptable behaviors to be successful in their work and work relationships including the ability to allocate their time efficiently and effectively and to understand how to handle their income, pay their bills on time, and invest for their future fiscal well-being.

Revised: [date]

Indicator: Number of students using critical thinking to participate in team problem-solving competitions

Indicator		Students	Students	
Number of CMS students participating in team Problem-Solving Competitions:	CMS	N 2008–09* Baseline	N 2009–10 Baseline**	Target 2010–11
CMS Math Counts CMS Future Problem Solvers	Total	76	75	≥75
Number of EPHS students participating in:	EPHS	N 2008–09* Baseline	N 2009–10 Baseline**	Target 2010–11
Debate Destination Imagination Future Problem Solvers Math Team Mock Trial Quiz Bowl Robotics Speech	Total	225	246	≥246
Community Education		N 2008–09* Baseline	N 2009–10 Baseline**	Target 2010–11
Students participating in: Destination Imagination (K–6) Chess Classes (K–6) Lego (K–6) Robotics (Grades 3–7) New for 2009–10: Crazy Chemworks Electronix Mad Science Classes	Total	434	518	≥518

*May include duplication of students

** As of April 28, 2010

> *Baseline Analysis:* Early data suggests that we should keep the target the same as these opportunities are focused on a unique population of students and we must test the reasonableness of growth in finite programs.

Indicator: Student Response on next Eden Prairie Student Survey
Time Management and Work Habits

- H.S. I feel adequately prepared to manage my time in order to demonstrate balance in my school, work, family, and other important activities. (1–5 Likert Scale)
- M.S. I consistently demonstrate the ability to manage my time in order to balance my school, family, and other activities and meet those obligations. (1–5 Likert Scale)
- E.S. Every time I have school work or family activities I can get both of them done on time. (1–5 Likert Scale)

Ethics

- H.S. When I have been unable to manage my time in order to meet school assignment deadlines I have not resorted to cheating. (Frequency Likert Scale)
- M.S. When I have been unable to manage my time in order to meet school assignment deadlines I have not resorted to cheating. (Frequency Likert Scale)
- E.S. Even when I don't understand an assignment at school I do not cheat. (Age-appropriate frequency scale)

Personal Financial Competency

- H.S. I fully understand the role of money and how to manage it through budgeting, checking, savings, and credit cards. (1–5 Likert Scale)
- M.S. I have an understanding of the role of money and how to manage it. (1–5 Likert Scale)
- E.S. I have an understanding of the role of money and how to save it for what I need. (Age-appropriate Likert Scale)

4.3   Develop and maintain positive relationships and demonstrate the
ability to work cooperatively with diverse groups of people.

Interpretation:

We interpret "develop and maintain positive relationships and demonstrate
the ability to work cooperatively with diverse groups of people" to mean that
students address learning and work challenges through demonstration of
constructive interpersonal skills. These skills include students demonstrating
an openness and willingness to collaborate with others even with apparent
or perceived barriers due to differences in racial, ethnic, cultural, physical, or
socio-economic backgrounds.

Revised: [date]

Indicator: Student self-report on treating one another with respect—Eden
Prairie Student Survey, [date]

Indicator		# of Students Agree	% of Students Agree
The percent of students self-reporting on the Eden Prairie Student Survey stating that students in their school treat one another with respect.	District Grade Levels	2008–09	2008–09 Baseline
Students in my school treat one another with respect. (Question #2 elementary, intermediate, and middle school surveys; Question #1 high school survey)	Elementary (grade 4)	452	70%
	Intermediate (grades 5–6)	841	63%
	Middle School (7–8)	677	52%
	High School (grades 9–12)	1,641	65%

Eden Prairie Student Survey, April 2009

Indicators: Student self-report on working well with people who are different from them.

COF Middle School Student Survey, [date]

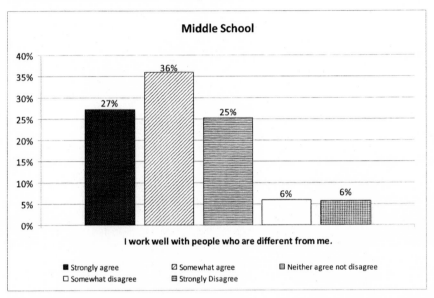

COF High School Student Survey, [date]

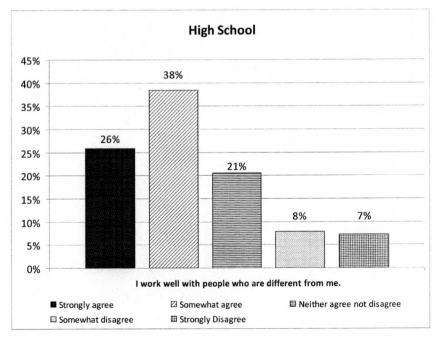

Baseline Analysis: Student survey data suggests that over 60 percent of our students believe that they have the ability to work and learn in a diverse world.

4.4   Have the resilience and self-confidence required to deal effectively with life's challenges.

Interpretation:

We interpret "have the resilience and self-confidence required to deal effectively with life's challenges" to mean that the student has the skills and capacity to recover readily from adversity and make changes to meet the challenges.

Revised: [date]

Indicator: Student Response on next Eden Prairie Student Survey

Resilience and Self-Confidence

- H.S. I feel I can effectively deal with life's challenges and recover and make changes to meet that challenge. (1–5 Likert Scale)
- M.S. I feel I can effectively deal with life's challenges and recover and make changes to meet that challenge. (1–5 Likert Scale)
- E.S. When I have a challenge that interrupts my learning, I can change and keep going. (Age-appropriate Likert Scale)

4.5   Possess the skills to manage and resolve conflict.

Interpretation:

We interpret "possess the skills to manage and resolve conflict" to mean that students take responsibility for their own behavior and when conflict occurs, employ effective strategies to resolve issues of disagreement, restore and strengthen relationships, and advocate on behalf of others.

Revised: [date]

Indicator: Student self-report on treating one another with respect

Eden Prairie Student Survey, [date]

Indicator		# of Students Agree	% of Students Agree
The percent of students self-reporting on the Eden Prairie Student Survey stating that students in their school treat one another with respect.	District Grade Levels	2008–09	2008–09 Baseline
Students in my school treat one another with respect. (Question #2 elementary, intermediate, and middle school surveys; Question #1 high school survey)	Elementary (grade 4)	452	70%
	Intermediate (grades 5–6)	841	63%
	Middle School (7–8)	677	52%
	High School (grades 9–12)	1,641	65%

Indicator: Student self-report on feeling safe at school
Minnesota Student Survey, Eden Prairie Data, [date]

Baseline Analysis: Data suggests that an indicator of success for those efforts is that our students feel and demonstrate respect among peers and staff that results in a learning environment that is both positive and safe.

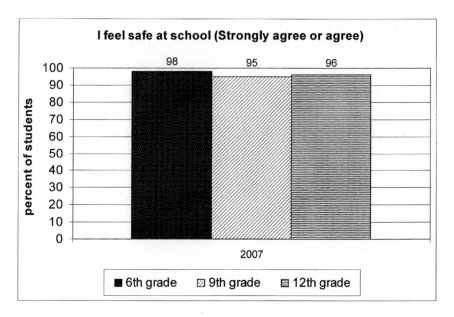

Indicator: Student Response on next Eden Prairie Student Survey
Conflict Resolution

- H.S. I feel that I can resolve conflicts and restore and strengthen relationships on behalf of myself and others. (Likert Scale)
- M.S. I feel that I can resolve conflicts and restore and strengthen relationships on behalf of myself and others. (Likert Scale)
- E.S. I feel that when my friends and I have a fight, I can settle it and keep my friendship. (Age-appropriate Likert Scale)

4.6   Be intrinsically motivated to learn, and

- Contribute to the common good of all by using their unique talents and interests, and
- Know and understand their own style of learning and how to apply it, and
- Identify their personal passions and pursue their evolving talents and interests.

Interpretation:

We interpret "be intrinsically motivated to learn" to mean that students are knowledgeable about themselves as learners and are able to apply their unique talents and interests toward the improvement of their own learning.

"Contribute to the common good of all" means that students use their academic, interpersonal, and other strengths to work for something beyond themselves that impacts their peers, school, community, or at the national or global levels.

We interpret "identify their personal passions and pursue their evolving talents and interests" to mean that students recognize their academic, interpersonal, and other strengths and seek and complete opportunities to excel in those areas.

Revised: [date]

Indicator: Student Self-Report on learning opportunities

Eden Prairie Student Survey, [date]

Indicator		# of Students Agree	% of Students Agree
The percent of students at the elementary, middle school, and high school levels self-reporting on the Eden Prairie Student Survey stating that they "strongly agree" and "somewhat agree" that they have multiple opportunities to learn based on their interests.	District Grade Levels	2008–09	2008–09 Baseline
I have an opportunity to learn new things that I'm interested in outside of the classroom. (Question #23 elementary survey; question 24 intermediate and middle school surveys)	Elementary (grade 4)	543	84%
	Intermediate (grades 5–6)	1,081	81%
	Middle School (7–8)	1,029	79%

(Continued)

Indicator		# of Students Agree	% of Students Agree
Eden Prairie Schools provides an instructional program providing opportunities for students to develop talents and interests in more specialized areas. (Question #33 high school survey)	High School (grades 9–12)	2,045	81%

Baseline Analysis: Data suggests that there are many options for students to understand their learning and abilities and to link their interests to required curriculum.

Indicator: Student Response on next Eden Prairie Student Survey
Knowledgeable about themselves as learners

- H.S. I feel I have a clear understanding of how I learn and can apply that knowledge to strengthen and improve my own learning. (1–5 Likert Scale)
- M.S. I feel I have a clear understanding of how I learn and can apply that knowledge to strengthen and improve my own learning. (1–5 Likert Scale)
- E.S. I feel I know how I learn and use it to become a stronger learner. (Age-appropriate Likert Scale)

Personal passions

- H.S. I can clearly identify my personal passions and talents and have taken advantage of opportunities to become excellent in my area of interest. (1–5 Likert Scale)
- M.S. I can clearly identify my personal passions and talents and have taken advantage of opportunities to become excellent in my area of interest. (1–5 Likert Scale)

- E.S. I have a good idea about my favorite things to do and find chances to learn more through school and in other places. (Age-appropriate Likert Scale)

Contribute to the common good

- H.S. I have had multiple opportunities and fully participate in contributing to the common good in and outside of school. (1–5 Likert Scale)
- M.S. I have had multiple opportunities and fully participate in contributing to the common good in and outside of school. (1–5 Likert Scale)
- E.S. I like giving to others and have participated in school and outside opportunities. (Age-appropriate Likert Scale)

4.7 Effectively use technology to access, communicate, and apply knowledge and to foster creativity.

Interpretation:
We interpret "effectively use technology to access, communicate, and apply knowledge and to foster creativity" to mean that students can use technology to globally access knowledge in multiple disciplines; evaluate the information sources to solve problems; use and creatively apply prior knowledge to new environments; and appropriately, ethically, and collaboratively share their learning in ever-changing technical environments.

Revised: [date]

Indicator: The percent of students at the elementary and secondary levels reporting the effect of technology on their ability to identify reliable resources, use those resources in multiple disciplines, and communicate them in a variety of ways.

Student Self-Report—COF Student Survey—Elementary [date]

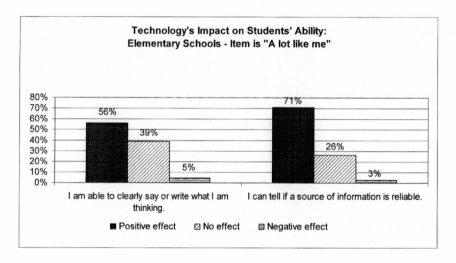

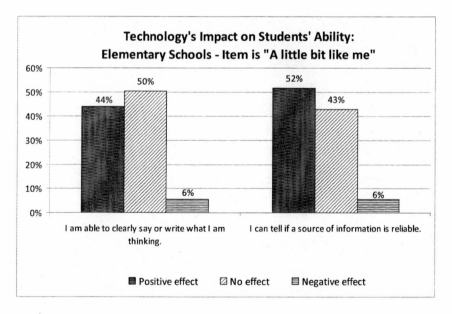

Indicator: Percent of middle and high school students reporting the effect of technology on their ability to communicate, identify reliable resources, and use their learning across subjects.

Student Self-Report—COF Student Survey—Middle School and High School, [date]

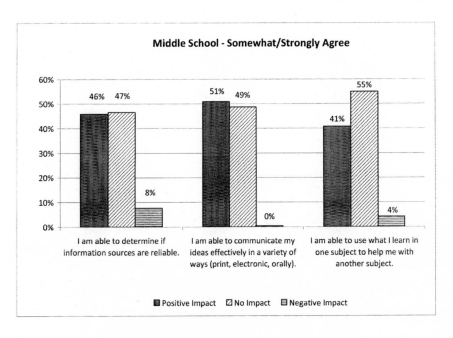

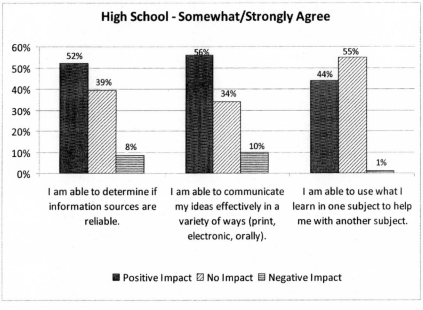

> *Baseline Analysis:* Student data suggests that the Classrooms of the Future technology work is having an impact on how students access, understand, and determine reliability of information that informs their learning.

Indicator: Student Response on next Eden Prairie Student Survey
Appropriately, ethically, and collaboratively share learning in changing technology environment

- H.S. I feel I have the skills and knowledge to use technology appropriately, understand ethics violations in its use, and work collaboratively with peers and faculty. (Likert Scale 1–5)
- M.S. I feel I have the skills and knowledge to use technology appropriately, understand ethics violations in its use, and work collaboratively with peers and faculty. (Likert Scale 1–5)
- E.S. I understand how to use technology and what the rules are for that use. (Age-appropriate Likert Scale)

> 4.8   Internalize and practice the core values of honesty, integrity, caring, trust, and respect.

Interpretation:
We interpret "internalize and practice the core values of honesty, integrity, caring, trust, and respect" to mean that students will become knowledgeable about themselves as people, and consistently communicate, act, and participate in school life with honor, compassion, and truth.

Revised: [date]
Core Values

- H.S. I understand the core values (honesty, integrity, caring, trust, and respect) and practice them routinely. (1–5 Likert Scale)

- M.S. I understand the core values (honesty, integrity, caring, trust, and respect) and practice them routinely. (1–5 Likert Scale)
- E.S. I understand the core values (honesty, integrity, caring, trust, and respect) and practice them every day. (Age-appropriate Likert Scale)

Adopted:

Revised:

Monitoring Method: Internal report

Monitoring Frequency: Annually
Eden Prairie, MN, School Board

Appendix D: Summative CEO Evaluation

EXECUTIVE SUMMARY

The board is pleased with the district's performance for the academic year (date). The superintendent's leadership during a time of higher academic standards and an uncertain financial future for public education is commendable.

The board recognizes that the superintendent's strengths have led to advancement on multiple fronts, including:

- Progress in academic achievement (R-2)
- Establishment of the Teacher Compensation Working Group (OE-5)
- Preparation of the Bond Package (OE-16)
- Initial High School Redesign efforts (R-3)
- Leadership and community visibility for public education and school finance (OE-10)

However, the district still faces significant challenges:

- Acceleration of the elimination of the achievement gap, particularly compared to peer school districts (R-2)
- Effectiveness of middle schools in preparing students for the rigor of high school (R-2)

- Implementation of the next phase of the High School Redesign Initiative (R-3)
- Improvement of customer service and treatment of stakeholders across the district (OE-3)

The board looks forward to another year of progress and is confident that the superintendent will continue to build on these strengths and will address the challenges identified in this appraisal.

I. RESULTS MONITORING:
Based upon the Results information provided, the board reaches the following conclusions relative to the superintendent's performance.

R-2 Academic Achievement
The board appreciates the significant gains made in the area of writing, the overall number of students passing state tests, the number of campuses recognized, and greater gains made by our district as compared to relative gains statewide.

However, the district needs to focus on academic achievement for all student groups in math and science. African American student achievement still lags behind too many subgroups, including economically disadvantaged and English Language Learners. The board's expectation is that math and science scores will improve and that African American students will exceed or match the state average at both the passing and the commended level.

The board is pleased with the additional focus on English Language Learners, Bilingual Education, and new initiatives for district's growing populations of immigrant students, including the International High School at ___. However, the district's Spanish test takers still lag behind the state's Spanish test takers. Hispanic students, who constitute over 55 percent of enrollment, are not succeeding at the same levels as Hispanic students statewide. The board's expectation is that Hispanic students will exceed or match the state average at both the passing and the commended level.

Our district must increase the number and percentage of students achieving at the commended level across all ethnic groups and income levels. The board's expectation is that students will match or exceed the state average for commended achievement in (date).

R-3 College and Career

The superintendent is to be commended for the initial steps to improve the high school experience for students based on the principles of rigor, relevance, relationships, and results. The district continues to build its strong partnership with our community college and has increased the number of students graduating. However, the district must accelerate its high school redesign efforts over the next twelve months and move from planning into action, including a meaningful public engagement process.

The district's focus on high schools cannot ignore the significant need to dramatically improve and upgrade the district's middle schools, especially in math and science.

R-7 Health and Safety

The board commends the superintendent for the progress in ensuring that more students understand the principles and practice of a healthy, active lifestyle, and his strong steps to provide better choices of nutritious food. However, the district must address the challenges of high school students' illegal use of drugs and alcohol. The board expects the superintendent to present analysis of the Signature Science Operational Assessment of the city Police Department, and after receiving direction from the board, implement the appropriate and necessary recommendations for improving campus safety and security.

Results Strengths:

R-2 Academic Achievement
- Improvement in performance in writing on state tests
- Greater overall district gains made by the district than statewide
- Increased percentages of students passing
- Number of campuses cited for acknowledgment
- Focus on bilingual education/creation of the international school

R-3 College and Career
- Establishment of community college and district partnership
- Increased number of students who graduated

- Continued improvement in the completion rate and the four-year graduation rate

R-7 Health and Safety
- Strong leadership in health, nutrition, and fitness

Results Areas of Focus:

R-2 Academic Achievement
- Need to improve academic achievement of all student groups with a focus on math and science
- African American student achievement lags behind too many student subgroups, including economically disadvantaged and English Language Learners
- Students lag behind the state average for all subgroups in achieving commended status
- Spanish test takers lag behind the state average for Spanish test takers

R-3 College and Career
- Implementation of High School Redesign and meaningful public engagement
- Improvement on middle school state tests performance and campus representation across the district

R-7 Health and Safety
- Analysis and implementation of Police Department audit
- Increased enforcement of drug and alcohol violations at campuses

II. OPERATIONAL EXPECTATIONS

Based upon the Operational Expectations information provided, the board reaches the following conclusions relative to the superintendent's performance:

Board is pleased with the superintendent's continued progress in addressing Operational Expectations as established through board policy. Of particular note is the high compliance rating reached throughout this evaluation period. The superintendent is to be commended on the stronger Human

Resource practices implemented, continued emphasis on financial stability, his commitment to district-wide curriculum alignment, and overall better communication with the board, staff, and stakeholders. The superintendent has also maintained a strong and positive visible presence in the community. While much success has been realized, there are some areas of focus the board wishes to emphasize, which if addressed, will bring about even better outcomes for the district.

Operational Expectations Strengths:
- Attained 90 percent full compliance on OE policies
- Implemented district-wide curriculum alignment (OE 12)
- Developed long-term facilities plan in support and for preparation of the 2004 Bond (OE 16)
- Created stronger Human Resources support (OE 5)
- Formation of the Teacher Compensation working group
- Improved teacher evaluation process
- Attained highest number of National Board Certified Teachers in state
- Achieved 100 percent administrative appraisals and 99.7 percent teacher appraisals completions
- Continued outstanding financial viability (OE 7)
- Maintained strong budget management and bond rating
- Allocated needed resources to support Results policies
- Established better communication (OE 10)
- Improved communication between board and superintendent
- Broadened communication efforts within the district and external audiences

Operational Expectations Areas of Focus:
- Respectful treatment of stakeholders at all levels throughout the district (OE 3)
- Expectation should be included in principal evaluation
- Acknowledgment of parents and community members as partners
- Expand circle of valued voices to deepen appreciation of diverse needs and outcomes of the community (OE 10)
- Follow up to issues raised with the study on high schools (OE 4)

- Create and maintain an effective facilities database with public access to nonclassified information of campus data (OE 16)
- Create a stronger organizational culture that encourages creative thinking and values open and honest communication (OE 4)

Signed_____   _____
         Board President   Date
Signed_____   _____
         Superintendent of Schools   Date

Glossary

Baseline: current performance measure that serves as the base against which future progress will be measured.

Benchmark: comparison of one organization's performance against other comparable organizations.

CEO: chief executive officer, superintendent, executive director—the board's sole link with the operational organization.

Clients: those persons who are served by your organization; those who receive the benefit of what you do.

Compliance: operating in a manner that meets the standards set by the Operational Expectations policies.

Data: subjective and objective information, statistics, facts, figures, records gathered to document compliance with operational standards and reasonable progress toward Results.

Formative: information intended to be used for internal, ongoing improvement as opposed to summative judgment.

Governance: the role played by a board of directors in its exercise of power and authority over an organization.

Governing Policy: written values identified by the board to govern four areas:

- *Governance Culture:* values by which the board will self-govern;
- *Board-CEO Relationship: values by which the board will relate to the CEO, defining delegation of authority and means for establishing CEO and organizational accountability;*
- *Operational Expectations: values that establish the standards for the organization's performance, including actions and conditions the board expects to exist and those to be avoided as the CEO makes operational decisions.*
- *Results: outcomes to be achieved for and by clients.*

Longitudinal: progress over time.

Monitoring: a process that establishes the current state of organizational performance. Operational Expectations monitoring reports document the state of compliance with Operational Expectations policies. Results monitoring reports establish whether reasonable progress has been made toward achieving Results.

Noncompliance: organizational failure to create operational conditions that meet the board's standards.

Organization: any entity created to fulfill owners' needs.

Owners: those whose support is necessary for the organization to survive; individuals whose lives are benefited, either directly or indirectly, by what the organization does.

Policy: the shared value of a board majority that drives action.

Preamble: the largest value of any policy; the opening statement. All other subparts of a policy are smaller, related values to the larger preamble statement.

Reasonable interpretation: statements intended to assure the board that the CEO understands the values represented by the board's policy statement and can apply that interpretation to organizational performance.

Reasonable person: a reasonable person is appropriately informed, capable, aware of the law, and fair-minded such that he is able to render a fair and unbiased decision.

Reasonable progress: organizational performance over time that represents progress from one point in time to another toward achieving the results defined by the board. The board, using the "reasonable person standard," according to approved indicators and performance targets developed by the CEO, ultimately defines reasonable progress.

Stakeholders: all individuals and groups of people who are, or might be, affected by the organization's performance; those who hold a stake in what the organization does.

Summative: the summation of, or conclusions reached about, prior monitoring of organizational performance.

Target: a measure of future or predicted performance forecast for each approved indicator.

About the Authors

Linda J. Dawson has more than thirty years of experience as a skilled author, consultant, coach, and facilitator with a career in teaching and administration, agency public relations, and association leadership. As an executive with the Colorado Association of School Boards, she developed cutting-edge governance training programs, which were widely regarded at the national level. The ensuing demand for her services in other states led to her decision to cofound the Aspen Group in 1993.

Linda attended Westmont College in Santa Barbara and graduated from Rockford College in Illinois. She was project director of a three-year project for the National School Boards Foundation on data-based decision making for boards. She is in demand as a consultant, speaker, trainer, and facilitator, both nationally and internationally. Linda is a widely published author in trade and association magazines. She is an accredited public relations professional (APR), a qualified Meyers Briggs Type Indicator consultant, certified in strategic planning, and trained by John Carver in his model of Policy Governance.®

Randy Quinn served for thirty years as executive director of two state school boards associations, in Alabama for nineteen years and in Colorado for eleven years. He has written more than four hundred articles for publication in various journals and has served on the boards of directors of numerous state and national organizations. He too benefited from the high visibility of the Colorado board training programs and cofounded the Aspen Group International in 1993 to extend his work throughout the United States and internationally.

Randy earned his undergraduate degree from Jacksonville State University in Alabama and his MA. and Ed.D. degrees from the University of Alabama. He too is a certified strategic planner and a graduate of John Carver's Policy Governance Academy.

The Aspen Group International, LLC, serves governing boards of all types, principally public and nonprofit boards. Aspen's special area of focus is public school boards, primarily due to the world from which both Linda and Randy came. The company also has worked with a range of other types of public and nonprofit boards, including cities, counties, self-insurance pools, conservation districts, elder-care organizations, and others.

Since forming the Aspen Group International in 1993, Linda and Randy have consulted with boards in most of the fifty states and others on three continents, including boards in Morocco, Korea, Borneo, Mexico, Singapore, and Canada.

Their work with boards "on the ground and in the trenches" led them to develop their own governing model variation in 2005. That course of action was taken primarily as a means to meet the specific needs of public boards, whose members face demands and pressures with which members of other types of boards are unfamiliar.

This book provides a straightforward overview of that model, which the authors believe to be the single best means by which public and nonprofit boards can provide effective leadership for the organizations they govern.